Daguerre Studio   Chicago, Ill.

With much love to my father & mother

Hendon Jr.

Hendon M. Harris, Jr.

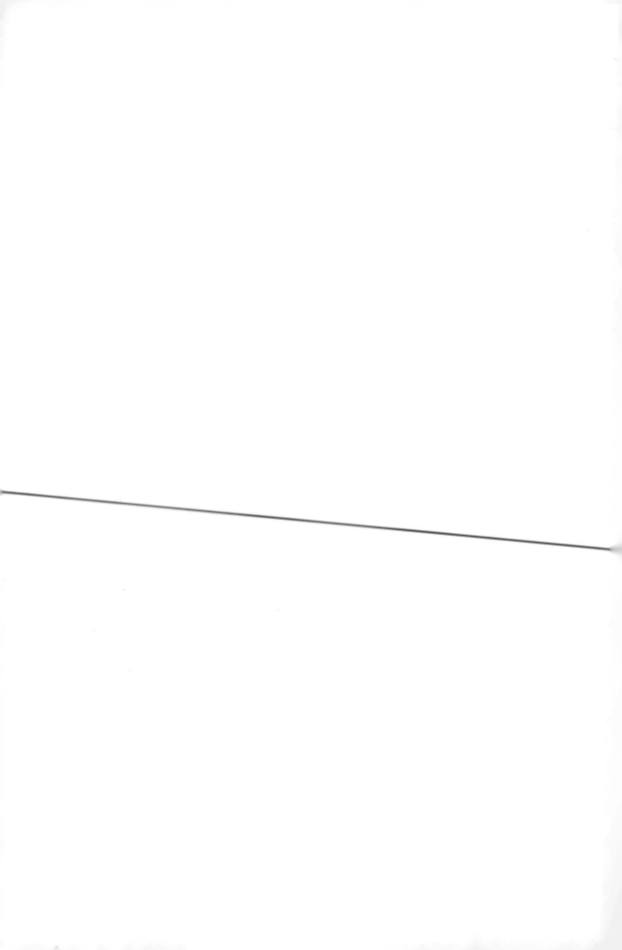

The Asiatic Fathers of America

Chinese Discovery & Colonization of Ancient America

Hendon M. Harris, Jr.

Edited and Abridged by Charlotte Harris Rees

The Asiatic Fathers of America
Chinese Discovery and Colonization of Ancient America
(Abridged Edition)

by Dr. Hendon M. Harris, Jr. (1916-1981)
Edited and Abridged by Charlotte Harris Rees

ISBN: 0-9786369-0-2

This book was originally published 1975
Wen Ho Printing Co., Ltd.
Taipei, Taiwan
Copyright on original book was
obtained 6/6/2003

Email: Harrismaps@msn.com

Warwick House Publishers
720 Court Street
Lynchburg, VA 24504

Contents

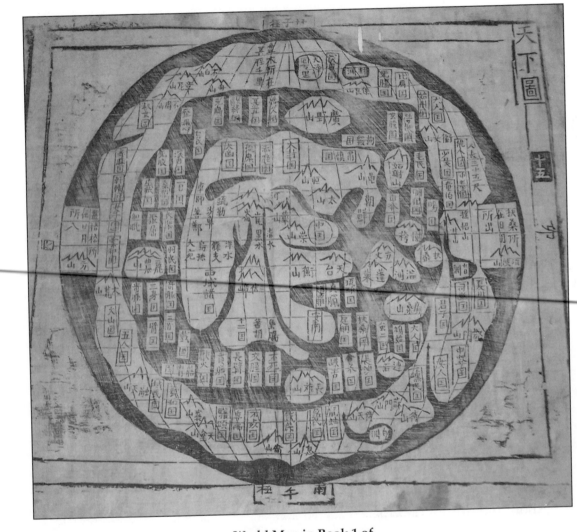

World Map in Book 1 of
Dr. Hendon Harris, Jr. Map Collection

古天下圖 何盛頓藏

A Chinese translation and clarification of the Harris Map

古天下圖
ANCIENT WORLD MAP
何盛頓藏
DR. HENDON HARRIS COLLECTION

World Map in Book 1 of
Dr. Hendon Harris Map Collection

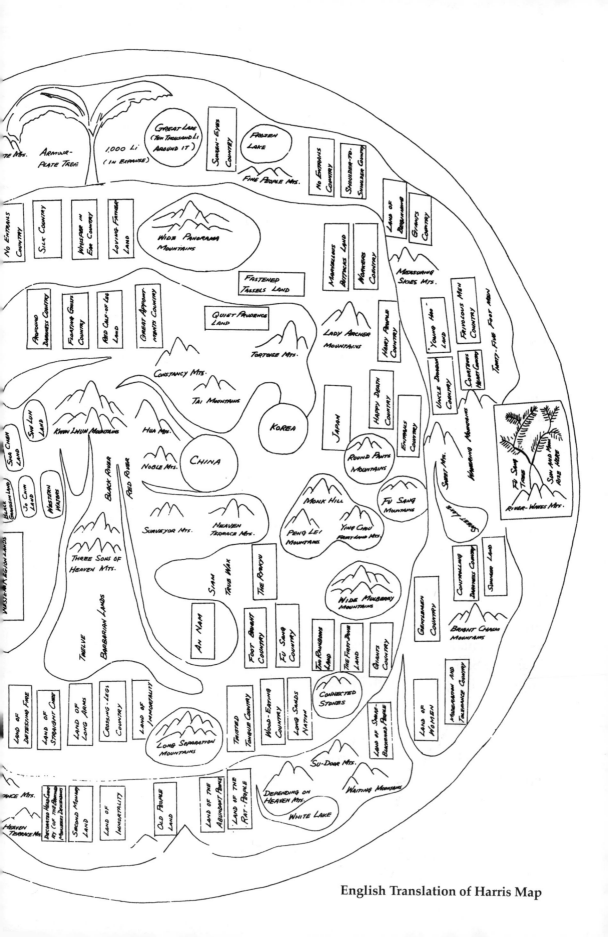

English Translation of Harris Map

Introduction by Charlotte Harris Rees

"The record of Asia is written into the stones of America
and into the bodies of its early people."
—Hendon M. Harris, Jr., 1975

Is it possible Asians visited and colonized the Americas long before Columbus? *National Geographic* states that some believe that when Columbus arrived there were already 30 million American Indians in North America.[1] Who were those Indians? From where did they come?

Losing a Lost Tribe (Simon Southerton) tells that *all* 175 Native American tribes from North, Central, and South America so far tested indicate founding DNA from Asia. That is corroborated by many other scientists who say that thousands of years ago "the Americas were initially settled by … immigrants from Asia."[2] Much other evidence indicates early presence of Asian culture in America. Multiple archeological digs reveal Chinese writings on Native American artifacts dating back over 3000 years. Some American Indian languages contain Chinese. Others have Japanese words.

How did the Indians come? Both *National Geographic*, March 2006, and *Encyclopedia Smithsonian* indicate that they came in boats. "A coastal migration route is now gaining more acceptance, rather than the older view of small bands moving on foot across the middle of the land bridge between Siberia and Alaska and into the continents. Emerging evidence suggests that people with boats moved along the Pacific coast into Alaska and northwestern Canada and eventually south to Peru and Chile. Sea routes would have provided abundant food resources and easier and faster movement than land routes."[3] The natural ocean currents would have carried them that way from Asia. **It is only logical that if one group survived the trip from Asia to America by sea at early dates, that over the years others could have followed.**

Ancient Chinese literature and the old Oriental maps my father found and associated with those writings indicate early Chinese trips to America. Throughout history, Chinese literature speaks of travels to a beautiful country to their east called Fu Sang (pronounced "foo song"). Today most Chinese believe Fu Sang was just myth. But was it?

My father, Dr. Hendon Harris, Jr., was born in China to missionary parents and later became a missionary himself. In 1972 he found an ancient Asian map in an antique shop in Korea. The map shows the location of Fu Sang, on a coast right where America should be. It was Father's ability to read classical Chinese, his knowledge of Chinese literature, and his familiarity with America that allowed him to understand the map when he first saw it.

Father subsequently wrote *The Asiatic Fathers of America*, which was published in Taiwan in 1975. It contains two books in one volume *The Chinese Discovery and Colonization of Ancient America* (2640 B.C. to 2200 B.C.) and *The Asiatic Kingdoms of America* (458 to 1000 A.D.). Father also contended that Chinese were not the only Asians to arrive on America's shores in early times. He was the first in recent times to correlate this style map with China, *The Shan Hai Jing*, Fu Sang, and America. However, his 783 page book is difficult reading. At the time it was published it was neither widely distributed nor accepted by many.

Father died suddenly of a stroke in 1981. For years his map collection lay in a box under my brother's bed. In early 2003, amid a flurry of worldwide debate about the possibility of Chinese in America before Columbus, I began my quest to find for myself the truth about Father's thesis and his maps. My brother, Hendon, and I took them to the Library of Congress. Leading experts have authenticated the maps themselves as genuine but some still question what they signify. The Library of Congress has expressed interest in acquiring the Dr. Hendon M. Harris, Jr. map collection.

Since Father's book was out of print for several years, in 2003 my six siblings and I were surprised when we were able to locate some copies of the original *The Asiatic Fathers of America* on the Internet. By 2005 the few remaining copies had risen in price as high as $160 per book. Now none are available. However, several recent books quote *The Asiatic Fathers of America*. On May 16, 2005, I gave a speech at the Library of Congress about my father's maps.

By publishing this abridged version of Father's book, I am allowing him to finish telling this timely story. I have shortened and rearranged Father's text but have kept it true to what he wrote. My few insertions are shown in brackets [ ]. Most of the pictures in this book were not in the original version. Dr. Cyclone Covey, Professor Emeritus of Wake Forest University and long-time scholar of the relationship of the *Shan Hai Jing* to America, has given priceless assistance and encouragement to me in this re-write. (Recent research on this topic and more pictures of the map collection will be in my upcoming book, *Fu Sang – The Forgotten Treasure*).

I realize that the information in this book raises many questions. I, myself, started out as a skeptic. As you read, try to keep an open mind to the possibilities.

—Charlotte Harris Rees

"Truth does not need to be defended.
If it is allowed to be free it will defend itself."
—John Milton

**Charlotte Harris Rees giving a speech about
the Dr. Hendon M. Harris, Jr. map collection
at the Library of Congress, May 15, 2005**

Foreword

We have proof that the Chinese discovered and colonized America thousands of years before the Europeans' arrival.

Approximately 4200 years ago after a great flood, the Chinese had lost their sense of direction. Therefore, the emperor found it necessary to send his astronomer Yu to survey the earth and reestablish the four directions. Yu sent Prince Y across the great eastern ocean, to the land of Fu Sang — literally "land to the east" (the ancient American continents). Prince Y and Yu determined the boundaries of America and other places, and afterwards wrote the *Shan Hai Jing*.

The *Shan Hai Jing (Book of Mountains and Seas)* is the world's oldest geography. It tells us of many countries in the ancient Americas. There are reports that Emperor Hwang-Ti (2640 B.C.) probably had sent expeditions or colonies to America. However, we can be certain that Chinese were in the Americas by around 2250 B.C.

I have found a map that confirms the 4200 year old account of the *Shan Hai Jing*. In fact, there are at least thirty similar old round maps in existence that vindicate and corroborate the report of the *Shan Hai Jing*. These world maps, of ancient origin, are in America, England, France, China, Korea, Japan, and in other countries. The *Shan Hai Jing* told of at least ten countries in America, which are found on my map—the Harris Fu Sang Map—and on the maps of similar origin which came from the original *Shan Hai Jing* map.

Proof that America is Fu Sang and that the fathers of the Fu Sang people are Chinese exists in:

1. The Record of the *Shan Hai Jing*, which describes the people, geography, and the animals.
2. The Record of the ancient Chinese commentaries on the *Shan Hai Jing*. The dates of these commentaries validate the age of the *Shan Hai Jing*.
3. The witness of the American Indians and their traditions and language.
4. The record of those scientists who have studied the blood and physical characteristics of the Chinese "Indian" tribes of North and South America.

5. The ancient round world maps that were previously misunderstood but which we now explain.
6. The Chinese Court Record (Kuen 327) in 501 A.D. telling of a trip originating in 458 A.D. to Fu Sang.

The Chinese arrived in the Americas both in 2200 B.C. and 458 A.D. by boat.

It is the purpose of this book to give sufficient proof of the realities of these amazing matters. The final result of these revolutionary discoveries will be the greater glory of China, East India, Japan, and Korea and a new respect for and the appreciation of the Indians of North, Central, and South America.

The material of this book is the result of a lifetime of effort. I have been around the world ten times. In India I sought information and in Pakistan and Bangladesh. In Hong Kong and Taiwan I looked for maps and proofs. I went to the British museum and traveled to Berlin to question the Germans.

From the time I was a boy in China until now I have collected information. In Holland, in Sumatra, in Macao, in Mexico I was searching ... searching ... searching. At Long Beach, California, and in Seoul, Korea, I received the greatest answers to my quest.

I am writing these lines in Taipei at the house of a Chinese friend. I am no longer young, and old age does not anymore seem a faraway time. I am grateful to those who loved and aided me, and to the great God of the heavens, without whose guidance all efforts would have been in vain.

It is my desire that as you consider the lovely long ago morning of Fu Sang, your soul be stirred with a new appreciation of the beauty of life and the innate possibilities of men...that you will hear the music of man's aspirations, deep in your spirit...and catch a glimpse of the excellent countenance of God.

I hope you will have a more sympathetic awareness of men of other persuasions and be drawn to the True Historian who works all things after His will.

—Hendon M. Harris

CHAPTER 1
Fu Sang

[Editor's Note: Somewhere between dreams and reality there is a special spot in everyone's longings. It is a wonderful and exciting place that we heard about in childhood. We wished that it were real but finally regretfully admitted that it probably was not. Today that dream is fulfilled for the Chinese. That place that they longed for—Fu Sang—was not just fantasy but was and is very real. There is too much evidence for us to dispute it any longer.]

Chinese sentiments about Fu Sang

The Chinese never completely lost faith in the existence of Fu Sang —a beautiful country across the Eastern Sea where the Fu tree grew to enormous heights was ever present in their imaginings, or rather memories.

The Chinese-America observatory—4600 years ago

Buddhist writer Kuan-Mei wrote in the Chinese *Long-Wei-Pi-Shu*, "It is in Fu Sang that Hwang-Ti's astronomers resided who were charged with the observation of the rising sun."[1] Hwang-Ti is the first historical sovereign of China. He reigned in the twenty-seventh century B.C.

If the Chinese claim that their first emperor had an observatory in America, I cannot see how knowledgeable scientists can deny it. Notice that the claim is modest enough. He does not claim that the king was manufacturing rockets. He simply claimed that the emperor had an observatory in America. Since the Egyptians had already built their pyramids by that date, should we doubt that the world's oldest continuous civilization could have had observatories in Fu Sang, made expeditions to America, and formed small colonies there nearly 3000 years before Christ?

Japan—not Fu Sang

The ancient Chinese maps call the countries of the north, Fu You, those of the south, Fu Nan, those of the west, Fu Lin, and finally, those of the east, Fu Sang. To the east of China there is no other extensive land than

America. If Japan has ever also been given this name of Fu Sang, it is because it is to the east of China, but the *Japanese Encyclopedia* says that it is NOT the true country of Fu Sang.[2]

The idea that Fu Sang was Japan only arose out of sheer frustration because of the Chinese inability and refusal in the last several centuries to remember where Fu Sang was.

Fu Sang situated to the east of Japan

In the preface of the *Ethnography of the Eastern Nations* by Ma Twan-lin it is distinctly said, "Japan is situated directly to the east of China, and Fu Sang is situated directly to the east of Japan."[3]

Fu Sang—3300 miles wide, bounded by vast oceans, with huge trees

Tong Fang Tso [who lived around third century B.C.], stated:

> At the east of the Eastern Sea, the shores of the country of Fu Sang are found. If, after landing upon these shores, the journey is continued by land toward the east for a distance of ten thousand li [a li is about 1/3 mile], a sea of blue color is reached, vast, immense, and boundless. The country of Fu Sang extends ten thousand li upon each of its sides. Great forests are found, filled with trees … the general appearance of the trees is similar to that of those which are called Chin (certain coniferous trees). They attain a height of several times ten thousand cubits, and it takes two thousand people to reach their arms around one of them.[4]

In this astonishing statement about Fu Sang (America) before the days of Jesus Christ on earth, we find:

1. Almost the exact measurement of the United States and Mexico. Tong Fan Tso tells us that it is 10,000 li from coast to coast across Fu Sang (3300 miles). On the other side of Fu Sang is a vast ocean. Fu Sang was a vast tract of land. It was not a little piece of Canada or a sliver below Alaska but was perceived to be an enormous land mass bounded by oceans.

2. The forests of the Pacific coast, where Eastern mariners first landed, contain such enormous trees that it is not difficult to imagine their size being exaggerated to fabulous proportions.

Edward Vining, in his book *Inglorious Columbus,* points out that the ancient Chinese had a remarkable knowledge of Fu Sang.[5]

Directions to Fu Sang

Li-Yen, a Chinese historian who lived in the seventh century spoke of a country called Fu Sang more than 40,000 li distant from China towards the East. He said that in order to reach it one should sail from the Coast of the Province of Leao-Tong, situated to the north of Peking. After traveling 12,000 li, one reaches Japan. After another 7,000 li the country of Wen-Shun is attained. Five thousand more li easterly leads to Da Han; Fu Sang is 20,000 li from Da Han.

Li-Yen made a serious mistake regarding the distance from China to Japan, or perhaps was misquoted. I believe Li was talking about a route that he has not been over himself but that other men were traveling in his day. He gave directions that were mainly correct about a route that was then only occasionally used.

Gift from Fu Sang—Arrowheads

Arrowheads were brought back to Emperor Yu and the Chinese court by the surveying parties returning from Fu Sang approximately 2205 B.C. [6] Henriette Mertz, in her book *Pale Ink,* tells us

> Chinese wanderings as early as 3000-2500 B.C. are known to have taken place in Siberia and across into Alaska. Stone knives, according to Dr. Creel [H. G. Creel, author of *The Birth of China*], found in China in all Neolithic stages and in Shang culture, are found among northern Asiatic tribes and among the Eskimos, but they do not occur in the Near East or in Europe.

> The Chinese themselves regard the stone implements as coming from that identical period. In the *Tribute to Yu (Yu King)* embodied in the *Shu King,* one of China's oldest documents, it is twice recorded that stone arrowheads were offered as tribute to the Emperor Yu. (2205 B.C.)

> It would appear to me that since the Chinese attribute [that] date to the stone implements, and they state in their records that arrowheads were first presented as a tribute to the Emperor Yu, that all of the various accounts tally as to date.[7]

We agree. Arrowheads were brought back to the Chinese Court by the surveying parties returning from "America." They are one of our great proofs of the Chinese colonization of Fu Sang.

Poems of Fu Sang

Ch'u Yuan who lived 343-277 B.C. wrote the celebrated poem "Li Sao." In these verses he travels to the ends of the universe in his thoughts. In the North he perceived the land of long days and long nights. In the South the boundless sea attracted his attention. In the West he perceived the sun descend and sink in a lake which has been assumed to be the Caspian Sea. Finally, in the East, in spite of the immensity of the Pacific Ocean, he caught a gleam of distant shores receiving the first rays of the dawn.[8] It is in a valley, in a land shaded by the Fu Sang tree.

Chiu Ko, who seems to have been an admirer of Ch'u Yuan, pictures himself as the Sun-God reluctantly leaving the magic loveliness of Fu Sang, to make the necessary circuit of heavens. It is a delightful work of imagination:

"The Lord of the East"

With a faint flush I start to come out of the East
Shining down on my threshold, Fu Sang.
As I urge my horses slowly forward,
The night sky brightens, and day has come.
I ride a dragon car and chariot on the thunder
With cloud-banners fluttering upon the wind.
I heave a long sigh as I start the ascent,
Reluctant to leave, and looking back longingly:
For the beauty and the music are so enchanting
The beholder, delighted, forgets that he must go…

The "T'ien Wen" (Heavenly Questions) fourth century B.C. inquires:

The Sun sets out from the Valley of Morning
      [reference to *Shan Hai Jing*]
And goes to rest in the Vale of Darkness.
From the dawn until the time of darkness,
How many miles is his journey?

And then, he proposes another poetical problem:

> When Yi shot down the suns [referred to in *Shan Hai Jing*],
> Why did the ravens shed their feathers?

About the year 156 B.C. Yen Chi penned these interesting lines:

> I can find no place in this muddy world,
> Go back and go forwards. I know not what I should do.
> My hat is so high that it cleaves the clouds:
> A long sword swings to and fro at my side
> My garments seem to constrict and cramp me
> The universe is not big enough for me to move in freedom
> To the right my coat-front brushes on Pu Chou Mountain
> To the left my sleeve catches on the Fu Sang tree.

None was more ambitious in fancy than Chiu Tan, who lived 77 B.C. In his poem "Yuan Yu" (The Far Off Journey) he roars across the Eastern Sea like a power boat:

> I threaded through the towering spray
> Making my way eastward,
> Tethered my six Dragons to the Fu Sang tree
> I summoned all the gods together at the revolving pole
> To marshal them I raised up the many colored rainbow
> I flung open God's palace and his heavenly park
> Ascended the Hanging Garden, whose brightness blinded me.

Fu Sang and heaven were far away, but life and its bitter realities were all too near. Sung Yu in his "Chao Hun" (Summons for the Soul to Return), written about 208 B.C., has these touching lines that use references from the *Shan Hai Jing*:

> O soul, come back! In the East you cannot abide.
> There are giants there, a thousand fathoms tall,
> Who seek only for souls to catch?
> And ten suns that come out together,
> Melting metal, dissolving stone
> The folks that live there can bear it
> But your soul would be consumed.
> Oh soul come back! In the East you cannot abide…

And also in the "Ta Chao" (The Great Summons) he pleads:

> O soul, go not to the East
> In the east is the great sea, where the swelling waters billow endlessly.
> And water dragons swim side by side, swiftly darting above and
> below
> It is clammy with rain and fog that glisten white and heavy.
> O soul, go not to the east, to the desolate Valley of Morning.[9]

Poems of Tu Fu (726 A.D.) (translated by Florence Ayscouth):

> When I came down from Ku Su Terrace, in the East,
> I had already arranged for a vessel to float on the sea:
> And until now resentment lingers in my mind
> That I did not succeed in exploring Fu Sang.

1. This is more than just a little poem about Fu Sang. It is evident that he had a deep longing to go to Fu Sang. I believe this longing was shared by hundreds of thousands of Chinese.

2. Tu Fu says in his poem that he had arranged for a vessel to float on the sea. The man is talking about something that he started to do and was interrupted. He said that resentment lingered in his mind over the abortive journey.

3. I feel that this poem is a strong proof that the Chinese of the eighth century accepted Fu Sang as a real and wonderful place and that if a man failed to go there he had failed to do something beautiful and desirable in his life.

A man from Fu Sang

In September 1883 Mr. Chung Nam Shan of San Francisco gave the following account: "Some fifty li east of Canton (in Kwang Tung Province) there is a temple named The Temple of Po Lo. Outside of the door stands a statue of a man who came from the Country of Fu Sang. Here he lived for some years, and here he finally died. After his death he was deified, and his statue placed at the door of the temple. He is represented as standing looking earnestly towards the East, with his right hand shading his eyes. At some later date a visitor to the temple wrote this stanza about him:

Where the Sun rises,
In the Land of Fu Sang.
There is my home.
Seeking glory and riches,
I came to the Kingdom
Of the Central Flower
Everywhere the cocks crow
And dogs bark,
The same in one place
As another
Everywhere the almond trees
Blossom the same.

The last two lines were intended to console a man who was homesick. The practical Chinese believed that one place is substantially the same as another. But notice … the man was deified. He must have been a very outstanding person. Notice how he grieved and longed for Fu Sang! What a lovely place it must have been! Notice how he shaded his eyes as he looked eastward. He knew that the land was far across the ocean. His grief was so great that the temple authorities remembered him mainly for his homesickness. It is not easy to grieve with all of one's heart over an imaginary place. The man from Fu Sang also proves that you could not only go there but that you could come back. The man from Fu Sang proves that the Chinese believed in this country and even had relationships with it not so very long ago, as the centuries move.

Both Asians and Europeans concede that Fu Sang was in America. I know of no major historian who claims that Fu Sang was not in America. Since this is true, the Fu Sang map is of extreme importance.

中國台灣台北中崙浸信会佈道所婦女会歡送何牧師轉回美叅 1954

Hendon and Marjorie Harris – Missionaries in Taiwan

CHAPTER 2
A Discussion of the *Shan Hai Jing*

The *Shan Hai Jing* is ancient geography

The *Shan Hai Jing (Book of the Mountains and Seas)* is claimed to be the most ancient geographical work which the Chinese possess, and is also thought by some to be the oldest geography of the world. "It originally contained thirty-two books or divisions, but in the fifth century A.D., they were reduced to eighteen."[1]

Henriette Mertz tells us: "The great Yu has been consigned four or five meandering dates but the Chinese credit him with the date of 2205 B.C. Yu was Minister of Public Works, serving under the Emperor Shun (2250 B.C.). Yu ... at the instigation of the Emperor Shun compiled the *Shan Hai King* [King and Jing are different spellings of the same word]."[2] (Yu later became emperor.)

The *Shan Hai Jing* gives detailed descriptions of the lands visited and the animals that were seen. Among the lands visited was Fu Sang—the land to the East. The *Shan Hai Jing* is a compilation of exploration reports containing much accurate historical information.

Mertz also stated: "For centuries Chinese scholars had studied this *Book of the Mountains and Seas*. This record of Yu was one of the books on which they were examined during the time of the great examinations of China."[3]

Chinese discussed the *Shan Hai Jing* throughout their history

"Confucius says"—According to the Chinese chroniclers, a copy of the *Shan Hai Jing* was found at the demolition of the house of Confucius [who lived 551-479 B.C.]. This copy was offered to Emperor Hiao Wu Ti by Kong Nagan-Kue, a descendant of the great philosopher. Taoist authors regard it as authentic.

Chapter 6 verse 1 of the *Confucian Analects* reads: (The Master said) "Truly straightforward was the historiographer Yu."

Tseu-hia, a disciple of Confucius, whose family name was Po-yang, wrote a commentary on the *Y King*, expressing himself in these terms in the *Kia-Yu* (the *Familiar Discourses of Confucius*): "During the reign of the Shang Dynasty (1831 to 1134 B.C.) mention was made of a *Book of the Mountains (Shan Jing)*.[4]

"Chao-shi lived during the reign of the Han Dynasty [202 B.C. - 9 A.D]. In a commentary on the *Chronicle of the Kingdoms of Wu and Yue* Chao-shi wrote that Y and Yu had composed the book *Shan Hai King*."[5]

In the *Consideration of the Western and Southern Kingdoms*, a book published during the dynasty of the later Han (25-220 A.D.) says: "*The Book of Mountains* contains a description of the world, from the country where the sun rises to the place where it sets."[6] It is obvious that the ancient authorities of the Far East looked upon this priceless work as truly descriptive of everything under heaven ... even as the Harris Fu Sang map states.

Wang-chong, lived during the reign of Hiao-ho-ti, who ascended the throne in 89 A.D. The work which contains his astronomical dissertations states: "The great Yu received the order to labor for the drainage of the waters: Y was charged to write the history of extraordinary events. These two men visited all the provinces, ascended the highest mountains, and visited the countries situated beyond the seas, and from all that they had seen and heard, they composed the *Shan Hai King*."[7] Some today think that Yu stayed home and ruled while he sent different teams to different lands. No one person visited them all.

Tso-sse who lived during the time of San Kuo (221 - 265 A.D.), mentions the *Shan Hai Jing* in a poem entitled "Wu-tu-fu" (Verse of the Five Capitals).

Minister Hsiu's report to a Chinese emperor said that Yu's party reached "mountains in the five directions internally" and "seas in the eight directions externally." On record in this book are the treasures and strange objects produced in exotic places; the places ... grasses and trees ... birds, animals ... different peoples of the remote countries beyond the four seas. Then Yu divided the world into nine chou administratively ... and he compiled the *Shan Hai Jing*.

The book entitled *Tsu-tse-yu* mentions "The *Shan Hai Jing* is full of doubtful statements, but who can affirm that the assertions which seem doubtful to us are absolutely false."

Yong Shun [Ming Dynasty 1368 - 1644] says that there was a *Shan Hai Jing* map. He said he half believed, half doubted, because the descriptions are so terribly strange. He says there were both the *Shan Hai Chronicle* and the Shan Hai Map at one time. Because the map is lost we can only half believe, says Yong.[8] From these statements we can determine that many Chinese had full trust in the fact that Yu had compiled reports based upon Chinese emissaries' visits to many foreign countries.

Now, if several Chinese writers of early centuries believed that the Great Yu had written the *Shan Hai Jing*, and if we find that what it says is true to ancient American history, I see no reason we should doubt what they believed.

Others in the past two centuries paid attention to the *Shan Hai Jing*

In the *Magazine of American History* for April 1883 there is a letter from the Rt. Rev. Channing M. Williams referring to the accounts of Fu Sang contained in the *Shan Hai Jing*.

Edward Vining's translation of the *Shan Hai Jing* (1885) states that Book Four contains the record of four surveys, from Canada south to Mexico that were made about 2250 B.C.

Vining stated, "A more careful examination of the original text of the *Shan Hai King* demonstrates beyond question that this 'Sacred Book of Geography' contains not only fabulous tales, such as might be expected in a work of such great antiquity, but also precise scientific statements from which the scholarly world can obtain much knowledge of the archaic period of the Chinese monarchy."[9]

Schlegel, taking the view that the *Shan Hai Jing* is the oldest traveler's guide in the world, attempted a number of identifications.[10] He had a difficult task because a proportion of the peoples mentioned are difficult to identify, such as winged men, viscera-less men, two-headed men and others. We may be dealing with landmark figures. The large figures or designs, discernable from planes in South America, may have a connection with the gods and symbols mentioned in the *Shan Hai Jing*. This may also be true of the mounds and large visible ancient symbols in the Eastern United States.

Henriette Mertz in her book *Pale Ink* charted the journeys of the Far East in Book IV of the *Shan Hai Jing* with mountains in North America.

Europeans of early times also held strange beliefs

The Europeans of the Middle Ages were as superstitious a people as ever decorated the globe. It is high time that the good folks who used to laugh at Asia be joshed a little themselves.

As late as the fourteenth century Europeans believed that there were women with ears so long that they could wrap themselves for the night with these natural ponchos. Having heard that Buddha had ears down to his shoulders, with typical European exaggeration, they converted them into blankets. The author has pictures of some of these eerie types as visualized by our ancestors. Europeans believed that there were people who had their eyes on their bodies. Men without faces, or with dogs' heads, and Amazons with one breast or none were found on the map. No story was too ridiculous to receive credence. Polyphemus, the giant with one eye, is a mild example of what our fathers believed to be reality.

Here are some typical beliefs of the early explorers who came to America. Acosta, Charlevoix, Sharp, and Water insisted that the peccary had its navel on its back. Herrera said that humming birds, when the rainy season is over and dry weather sets in, fasten themselves to trees by their beaks and soon die of hunger. In the following year when the rains came they were resurrected. Purchas mentions winged serpents, and tribes of Indians who lived to be more than 300 years of age. Hernandez told of a two-headed serpent and gave pictures of the flying dragon of America. Pigafetta, Von Nord, Hawkins, DeWeert and others all agreed that Patagonia was inhabited by giants. Their only point of disagreement was whether the average height was eight or ten feet. It would be wrong to say that Norsemen were omitted from the list of true believers. They tell of the marvelous unipeds.

[In summary: Books of antiquity might be expected to contain some fabulous tales as the *Shan Hai Jing* does. It was probably recording the beliefs of the countries visited. However, there is more than enough truth written in the *Shan Hai Jing* to convince us that the Chinese actually did make it to America at an early date. The English translation of part of the *Shan Hai Jing* is in the addendum to this book.]

Dr. Hendon Harris, Jr. – Missionary work in Taiwan

CHAPTER 3

The Strait Facts – They Came by Sea

The Passage of the Bering Strait

One of our dearest conceptions, myths, and blind beliefs in America is that the "Indians" came over by way of the Bering Strait. It is a beautiful theory destined to be cruelly destroyed by facts.

In the first place I believe that man has possessed boats and rafts since at least Noah's flood. Man has loved to paddle on the water since remotest antiquity. Man loves to be lazy, when laziness is possible, and so he is always looking for a ride on a camel or a Cadillac, in a VW, or a boat. He does NOT keep coming by way of an almost impossible path when better ways can be employed.

Men do not wade through three thousand miles of snow and bitter winds in order to make a dangerous crossing that will mark them the first visitors in the New World. In other words, primitive man was looking for food not fame. The Bering Strait is the most unlikely place to find either.

In order to make their Bering hypotheses seem more plausible, some say that Asia and Alaska were once joined. But when, and where, and why? And others claim that Hawaiian weather once prevailed at the Arctic Circle. I hope it did. But if so, it was before our time and did us no good.

The real answer is the Japan Current. It was on this helpful stream that men rode merrily down to the Los Angeles area. The Bering Strait boys either died of starvation or old age. Only the lazy (the drifters from Asia) came through. Ever since I first rode the Japan Current on a Japanese ship to America I have preferred being carried to walking. (I was only 16 months old at the time, but the principle still holds.) I believe the first immigrants to America had similar feelings.

The Japan Current [Kamchatka]

There are marvelous rivers in the ocean. One of these is the Gulf Stream which flows along the Atlantic coast. The same is true of the Japan Current. Vining comments:

The great thermal ocean current, analogous to the Atlantic Gulf Stream, which commencing in the equatorial regions near the Asiatic continent flows northward along the Japan and Kurilian Islands, and then, bearing eastward, divides itself into two streams. One of these, following the main direction of the Asiatic coast, passes through the Strait of Bering, and enters the Arctic Ocean; while the other and the principal current, flowing eastward, and skirting the southern shores of the Aleutian Islands, reaches the northwest coast of America, where it flows southward along the shores of Oregon and California where it finally disappears.

The current or thermal river in the midst of the ocean would constantly tend to throw Asians from Japan and Kamchatka upon the Aleutian Islands, from which their gradual progress eastward to America would become assured. It is common at the present time to find trunks of camphor-wood trees from the coast of China and Japan upon the shores of the islands of the easternmost of the Aleutian chain, carried there by this ocean current. It also explains the agency by which a disabled Japanese junk with its crew was borne directly to the shores of California … Another remarkable effect produced by this warm ocean current is the temperate climate which it bestows upon this chain of islands, and upon the northwest coast of America. These considerations assure us of a second possible route of communication, besides the Strait of Bering, between the Asiatic and American continents.

The "Histoire de Kamchatka" mentions a report that a Japanese vessel was wrecked upon Kituy, one of the Kurile Islands. M. Pinart states that a number of Japanese junks, borne by the currents and probably by the great Japanese current … "Black Stream," have been shipwrecked upon the Aleutian Islands. One such case having occurred in 1871; thus showing that if a boat were merely allowed to drift with the current along the eastern shore of Asia, it would pass by the way of the Kurile and Aleutian Islands, and, if not stopped by these, would soon drift to the American coast.[1]

This same trip across the ocean whether in the Japan Current or another is still possible today. This account was in the August 26, 1962, *Independent Press Telegram*, Long Beach, California.

A briney trio of seafaring adventurers, including a pretty Australian nurse from New Guinea, docked at Terminal Island Saturday after a 57-day, non-stop trip from Yokahama, Japan, in a 39-foot sailing schooner. Skipper Joseph Pachernegg, age 39, a native of Australia and former German submarine pilot, declared, "The trip was so easy that an old woman in a rocking chair could have done it."

It is said that the little ship followed the 43rd Parallel all the way across. The crew managed to catch fish almost every day of the journey to supplement their food supply.

The navigational abilities of the ancient Chinese seamen

By 2600 B.C. the Chinese had a compass. We are assured by Joseph Needham in his book *Clerks and Craftsmen in China and the West* that:

> Chinese pilots in the period of primitive navigation certainly made use of all the usual aids which were known in ancient times. Like sailors in other civilizations these ancient pilots were observant men, men who took soundings, noted sea-bottom samples, marked the prevailing winds and currents and recorded depths, anchorages, landmarks and tides—nor did they forget to use the services of shore-sighting birds. The stars were extremely important. By night they could tell the time by the circumpolar and the culminations or risings of stars, gaining an idea of their latitude by rough assessment of the height of the pole seen against masts and rigging. By day the varying relations of ecliptic and horizon helped them to construct their wind-rose. Time and distance estimation was still extremely crude, no more than a count of day and night watches with a guess at the way made good.

> There is special reason however for believing that the ancient Chinese mariners were good star clerks. Chang Heng, the great astronomer, wrote in *Ling Hsien* (+118): "There are in all 2500 greater stars, not including those which the sea people observe." There has been doubt as to how the expression "hai jen" [sea people] should be translated here but very probably it meant sailors. There are seven or eight [Chinese mariners' manuals] all finished before the end of the 1st century. Their skills were doubtless undifferentiated and it would be impossible to disentangle them from the components which today we should call astrology, astronomy, stellar navigation, weather prediction, and the lore of winds, currents and landfalls— all the more since … these elements were still wholly confused down to the end of the seventeenth century in Europe.[2]

By 1137 A.D. Chinese knew both longitude and latitude. A Chinese map carved in stone (Yu Chi Fu) dated to 1137 was discovered based on advanced cartography which included spherical trigonometry and the use of effective instruments for determining latitudes and longitudes.[3]

The early Chinese had fine big ships

By 412 A.D. Fa Hien's ship could take 200 passengers plus 200 crew. Marco Polo also mentioned large Chinese ships with tenders.

The outstanding calligrapher Stephen Wu found in his researches that Yong Su of the Sui Dynasty (*581-617 A.D.*) was a very talented engineer. He built ships called the Five-Teeth class ships. These ships had five floors. They were warships and could carry 800 archers, soldiers, and sailors.

Yong Su also designed the smaller Yellow Dragon craft which carried 100 soldiers, and acted as destroyer escorts for the larger ships of the line. This was about the year 587 A.D.[4] Yong Su built his ships more than 100 feet high at Yung An. Ibn Batuta says the largest class of Chinese junk had a crew of 1000 men (600 mariners and 400 soldiers).[5]

Evidence of transpacific voyages

There is much evidence that repeated boat trips were made between Asia and the Americas before Columbus. Corn, tobacco, and cochineal that originated in the Americas were found to have existed in Asia before Columbus.

Several items that originated in Asia were found in the Americas. Chickens found in the Americas were of Asian bantam types of India and Japan. Pottery with oriental designs recurred widely in the Americas, some even with Chinese characters [writing] on them.

There has been great debate about cotton in America. Nearly every earnest student of early America has wrestled with the stubborn problem of the odd American cotton of the pre-Columbian era.

There is wild cotton native to the Americas. Its germ cells contain 13 small chromosomes. The germ cells of Old World cotton in both the wild and domesticated form bear 13 large chromosomes. However, the seeds of domesticated Fu Sang cotton contained 26 chromosomes, 13 of them large and 13 small. This was a mystery and a problem enough to madden anti-diffusionists. If one is to be a loyal anti-diffusionist, he must get all his supplies from the home ground. Here was a disobedient undisciplined plant that was half Asiatic and half American. This hybrid was enough to ruin all the joys of historic research. Olivia Vlahos, who wrote *Indian Cultures in America*, attacks this problem with courage but asks "When, and how?"[6]

The Asiatic Waves

When an island or continent is being attacked, it is customary to send soldiers ashore in several successive parties or waves. So it was with the Asiatic settlements and conquests of the new world.

Many of these waves were purely accidental. Let us imagine a Japanese boat of the third century A.D. with seven men on board fishing off the coast of Honshu. A violent storm comes up. Despite their most frantic efforts they are blown northwards by fierce winds and the strong current. With great skill they manage to keep alive, but they see to their despair that they are being carried to the north and east.

After four weeks of storm and stress they find themselves off a strange and beautiful coast. They are nearly mad from thirst and hunger, but now their hopes revive, and they crawl ashore.

About one month later five girls disappear from a nearby Indian village. It is useless to try to find them but there are rumors that a new cunning gang is in the neighborhood who are very good in fishing and who carry long spears made from poles and who wear armor made of reeds. And so, a new tribe is born. One of the Asiatic waves has come ashore.

Another type of wave would be deliberate. Perhaps a Chinese governor would send an expedition to see if the fabled Fu Sang was as fair and productive as the stories said. Maybe great gain would come to the sponsors. But alas, the ship was damaged on its way across the Pacific, and the current was much more favorable to those coming in than to those returning. So the members of the party stayed by choice or necessity. Another wave had come ashore.

We frequently hear of Japanese shipwrecks off the American coast. In one century there were at least a hundred Japanese ships lost along the American shore line. Some shipwrecks may have been Korean. These shipwrecks continue until today.

There are legends from both China and Japan of boatloads of thousands who sailed out into the Pacific Ocean and never returned. According to Henriette Mertz, one large group of Chinese left around 219 B.C. and a group of Japanese around 100 A.D.[7]

The wide range of dates indicated by the various Asiatic traits which must have been introduced in the course of contacts shows that from 700 B.C. on, regular transpacific voyages were taking place. The sequence was never really interrupted until the ninth or perhaps tenth century A.D. Why it finally ended we do not know.

Book burnings affected knowledge of the sea ways

Vining believed that the general burning of books in China in 213 B.C. was not nearly as destructive as imagined[8] but did cause a considerable diminution of knowledge. However, I believe there can be little doubt that the burnings struck a severe blow followed by a sharp regression in world geography, science, astronomy, nautical science and other important areas. Without these lost burned books, most people seem to have forgotten the sea ways to Fu Sang.

Vining says "The Chinese in very ancient times were possessed of ideas more just and extensive, regarding a multitude of subjects, than the Chinese of the following centuries. To reach reliable accounts it is necessary to go back as far as possible into that antiquity which, perhaps, there is good reason for vaunting so highly."[9]

On the American front similar book burnings took place. The European priests reputedly destroyed every bit of pre-conquest writing they could get their hands on in the early days. According to the great American Indian historian Ixtlilxochitl, the Mexicans originally had a *Divine Book* or *Teoamoxtl*. It was composed by a Tezcucan doctor, named Hue Huematzin (probably Hui Shan himself) supposedly toward the close of the seventh century. It gave an account of the migrations of his nation from Asia, of the various stations on the journey, of their social and religious institutions, their science, and arts. It has never been seen by a European. A copy is said to have been in the possession of the Tezcucan chronicler on the taking of the capital. Prescott says that if reports be true the Tezcucans had an important compilation of books they had gotten from the Toltecs.[10]

Dr. Hendon M. Harris, Jr. Map Collection
World Map Book 6

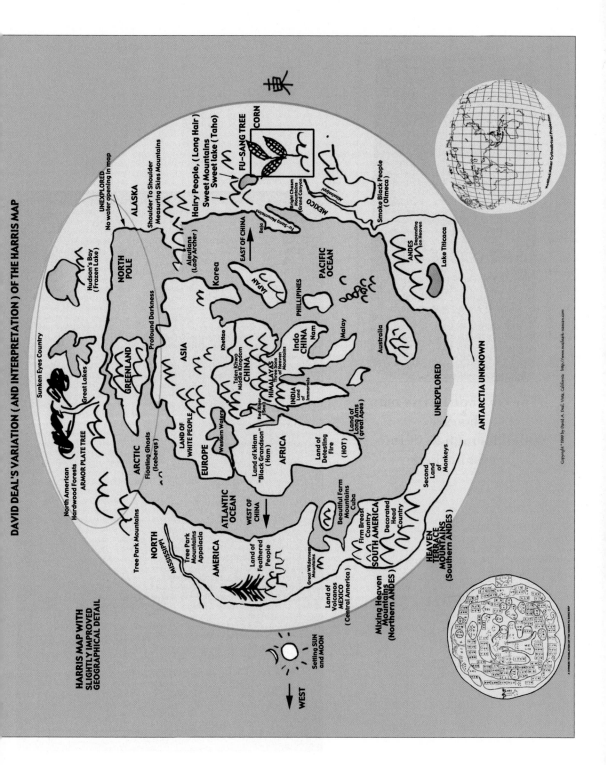

David Deal's interpretation of Harris map

The cover of Harris map
book 4
(small enough to fit into a
vest pocket)

One map in book 4 partially unfolded
(each map folds separately into the book)

One of the Korean maps in map book 4.
Details about the area are in the bottom section of the map.

World Map in Book 5 — Dr. Hendon M. Harris, Jr. Collection

CHAPTER 4
Harris Finds a Map

In August of 1972 I found it necessary to pass through Seoul, Korea. Rising in the morning, I thought I would use my time by visiting antique shops. In a swift reconnaissance mission I swept through about twenty-five establishments and was about to return to my hotel … when I entered one last place. I asked the proprietor if he had any books or pictures. He replied: "Would you be interested in a book of old maps?"

When I opened the book I noticed it contained many ancient cartographic sketches. There was also a very strange-looking map of Japan that must have been made at an extraordinarily early date. And then … I opened the last map … and had to control myself, to keep from trembling. It was very old and unusual. "Everything Under Heaven" was the title. It was terribly odd. China and Korea took up the center of the world. North of Japan Asia arched round to Alaska. Down the North American coast it was marked "Fu Sang."

I became weak. I was forced to sit down….

Vining said of Fu Sang: "Chinese investigators interested in antiquarian researches never allowed this land, which had been once described with so many details, to be forgotten. Chinese scholars have mentioned it frequently in their works, and have even given it a place in their maps."[1] So they did indeed.

Some facts and qualities of the Harris "Everything Under Heaven" (World) Map

- The Harris "Everything Under Heaven" (World) Map is round and is written in classical Chinese. While the map is in some respects wrong, in most essential respects it is so continually right that we can immediately tell authenticity. Both its great age, and the actual journeys of the makers of this map are authenticated. We know that as early as the seventh century B.C. the Babylonians had round maps. This "Everything Under Heaven" map seems to date back to earlier maps of the third millennium B.C. We know that the ancient Chinese regarded their country as the center of the world, and in this odd map China, Korea, and Annam [Vietnam] take up the center of the world.

The Central Kingdom [China] is at the center. Around the edge of the world runs a thin circle of land. From Chinese perspective the name Central Kingdom was not boasting, but fact.

- East and West on the map are clearly indicated. On the left side of the map is a caption that states "The Sun and Moon set here." On the right side of the map are captions stating "Fu Sang Tree" and "Sun and Moon rise here." Korea and Japan are shown east of China. We cannot be mistaken as to our directions, or to the main locations of the map.

- Due North of China is the Great Lake, which we believe to believe to be Baikal and also a Frozen Lake. North is also Sunken-Eyes Land, which must imply the early European settlements of Siberia. I consider this designation of ancient Siberia as non-Chinese, one of the great proofs of the authenticity of the map itself. No Chinese imposter would have dared to say Siberia was not Chinese, if he sought to maintain the favor of his associates.

The right side of the map

Fu Sang – Three times we see the land on the extreme right (East) of the map designated Fu Sang. Fu Sang Mountains, Fu Sang Forest and Fu Sang Continent appear indicated. We can have no doubt we are dealing with west coast America.

Land of Beginning is Alaska. Since Fu Sang is the center, the eastern side of the map is plainly the beginning of the Fu Sang area.

Hairy People Land – near Land of Beginning – these are probably the Eskimos.

Equal to Heaven Mountain (Measuring Skies Mountain) is probably Mt. McKinley—the highest peak in North America.

Chasm of the Bright Mountains is at the spot where the Grand Canyon of the Colorado is found. (See chapter 7) Several hundred miles east of modern Los Angeles are the Low Bright Mountains. The only place in the world where there are famous mountains that are very bright and yet beneath the earth's surface are the Low Bright Mountains. Their presence on the map is immediate confirmation of the 4,200-year-old stories about Fu Sang in the Chinese *Book of the Mountains and the Seas – The Shan Hai Jing*. Every person who has visited the place where the mountains are hidden in the bowels of the earth will recognize this place as the Grand Canyon. Here is the river that went to form the beautiful gulf told about so long ago by the Chinese.

Gentlemen Country – We find this land in the area between modern Los Angeles and San Francisco. This is a confirmation of the *Shan Hai Jing*, which spoke before of a Country of Refined Gentlemen who had excellent manners and a high degree of civilization.

The Land of Women (see chapter 15) is placed near the spot where the Spanish Conquistadors were searching for them. It is exactly where Hui Shan told the Chinese Ling Dynasty court in 502 A.D. they were located.

The Gulf of Baja is in its proper place. The fact that it is reversed only gives further assurance of the extremely early date of the original of this map.

White Lake at Cha Hill (Mexico plateau) is just at the place we would expect. From our comparison of White Lake with the maps made by others, we can see at once that the Harris Fu Sang map was made at an early time, when the lake was still large and in one piece. This would have been before it was fragmented into three or more lakes, as it was, by the time of the Aztecs.

Professor Ignacio Bernal in his "Mexico Before Cortez" presents four maps of the Mexican Lake in Mexico City valley before and after its fragmentation and shrinking into smaller disappearing lakes. He shows the lake as it was in the prehistoric, Aztec, 1800 A. D., and 1889 A.D. periods, gradually shriveling and disappearing.

Decorated Head Country (see chapter 14) is found in Yucatan. The French copy of this map even shows Yucatan on the Pacific with the "Decorated Head" people there. The long and decorated heads are exactly what were found among the leadership class in Maya land.

The Land of Hsi and Ho – the astronomers of China (see chapters 8 and 9) – is in Central America. It fits perfectly with the traditions and history of that land.

The left side of the map

A Chinese friend pointed out to me that we must not be surprised at the names given to many European countries. The Chinese are a realistic people and intensely conscious of "differences." They think of us as Sunken-eyes people because that is exactly what we are to the eyes-forward people of the Far East.

Land of Arms might be a country where the sleeves ballooned out.

Strange Forearm Land might be a region where heavy brass bracelets were worn, or blue tattooing.

One-Eye Land might be the legendary home of Polyphemus in whom the ancient Greeks devoutly believed.

Firm Breast Land was perhaps named after the admirable physiques of Minoan ladies and statuary.

Who can find fault with the poetry of The Beautiful Farmer Mountains? To a nation where agriculture was the first of professions this was praise indeed.

Ancient Country is a respectful designation from a land that honored the archaic.

The Feathered People Land is not surprising. Our own ladies were literally swooping with feathers at one time. Chinese have been gifted at feather work since early epochs.

I am saying this to demonstrate that the names rather than being ridiculous are natural and often commendatory. Consider the fresh sweetness of Maiden Country, the elfin charm of Floating Ghosts Land (in which all European travelers devoutly believed, and so the Chinese would include it).[2]

Three-Head-Land may have been ruled by three brothers or had three famous busts over its city gate. The Chinese would never forget Bowing Assembly Land where the citizens were as dignified and respectful to the gods as themselves.

No Entrails Land may have been "gutless wonders" who had no stomach for fighting and who lacked intestinal fortitude. Or perhaps, they were extremely modest about eating or defecating in the presence of others which might arouse suspicions that they were truly without bowels. I remember eating a small cake in the presence of some Chinese children. I chewed it, but didn't swallow. The kids watched in fascination. Here was something new, digestion through osmosis. When I finally swallowed the food and they saw my Adam's apple in action, they let out a shout of joy and derision. I was just another person like themselves. (A lady once told me that on a trip to Hopi land, the Hopi girls were not sure she wasn't a spirit, until they were given proof in the restroom.)

Is there anything wrong with the <u>Land of Great Happiness</u>...where lovers were true and men repaid debts? Where children and their parents had a mutually happy relationship.

<u>The Land of Everlasting Jute</u> sounds like a pleasant place for rope makers.

<u>Whisper-in-ear Nation</u> was certainly more desirable than folks who bellow.

<u>All-witches Land</u> still exists, they say. One is reminded of the man who said to Groucho Marx, "I would like to say goodbye to your wife," and he replied, "Who wouldn't?"

<u>Plowing Monkey Land</u> makes a lot of sense to a man who has always believed hard work was for the animals. Perhaps it was a prominent statue or a play on words.

What is funny about the socialistic country of <u>Mutual Help</u>? Is <u>Cloud-Peace-Land</u> lovely rather than odd? Is it not possible that the matriarchy of <u>Female Country</u> actually existed?

I believe that there was a <u>Land of White People</u>. It is believable that there was a <u>No-Leisure Land</u> even before the Czar invented the delights of the Siberian salt mines.

<u>Red Calf of Leg Land</u> could be a designation of a country where people wore scarlet puttees on their limbs.

We have pointed out these things to show the unreasonableness of those early critics who dismissed the Chinese world maps as ridiculous. In fact, considering the wild notions that existed in pre-Christian Europe concerning the rest of the world, the names are realistic and appropriate.

- Each Harris Fu Sang Map is part of a book of maps that go back not only into early Chinese but also early Korean times. The authenticity of the Harris Map rests not on itself alone, but on the entire family or compilation of maps in the Harris Map books.

- The original map, of which the Harris map is an old, faithful copy, runs back into remote antiquity. There are several copies (in museums around the world, but apparently up to now were misunderstood or misinterpreted). Since there are several of them there is little possibility of fraud or collusion. Even if one did not accept the authenticity of the Harris Map, what should he do with the other maps in the British Museum, in Paris, in Tokyo and in Korea that give nearly an identical witness? They are either all true or all false, because their witness and placement of tribes and nations is almost exactly the same.

Why was the World Map not interpreted before?

It seems truly amazing that the obvious confirmation which the ancient world maps give to the *Shan Hai Jing* story should have been overlooked by wise and knowledgeable savants for hundreds of years. It might well be wondered how such a colossal error could have taken place … that is, the failure to do the obvious and see whether the *Shan Hai Jing* (the world's oldest geography) is proven true by the ancient maps.

There are several reasons…and we shall name some of them:

- The Chinese had themselves "given-up" the *Shan Hai Jing* as too absurd for credence and did not look for Fu Sang in America, but instead searched for it in the Orient. It is no wonder they did not find it. They broke their own hearts by not following the instructions of the ancients who told them as plain as the rabbit in the moon, that Fu Sang was beyond the Eastern Sea. [While Americans see a man in the moon, Chinese see a rabbit.]

- The China experts around the world could not understand either the *Shan Hai Jing* or the maps because most of them had little faith in Chinese records, and knew little if anything of the Chinese language … with some notable exceptions.

- The Japanese, American, German, British and other students of Sinology have generally taken a skeptical follow-the-leader attitude of distrust toward ancient Chinese records. I was simple enough to assume that their ancient records were true, and that the Buddhist chronicles were reliable. I was richly rewarded for my faith and confidence. I have nowhere seen proof that Buddhism or Asiatic ancestry made one's ecclesiastical or national records unworthy of credence.

- There is generally present among "scientists" the basic assumption that European records are more trustworthy than Asiatic ones. Being born in China, I did NOT take this attitude. It is a wrong approach, now beginning to change. Joseph Needham of Britain proved that the Chinese were probably the scientific leaders of the world in early times.

- Since scientists and archaeologists had not correlated American pre-Columbian history with the facts of Asian primacy in America ... how could they be expected to correlate the *Shan Hai Jing* with the map? If they followed Klaproth and supposed Japan was Fu Sang, how could they be expected to grasp Truth when present before their eyes?

- Persons such as Hapgood, Mertz, and Vining and the great French Fu Sang exponents of two centuries ago must have come close ... because of their good sense and scholarship, to finding the truths that the maps and the *Shan Hai Jing* jointly prove. But there was a commonly held mistaken impression that the rectangular boxes on the map extending from the ring continent into the ocean are islands. (I believe they are just legends describing the mainland.) That wrong impression made proper interpretation impossible. Perhaps this also led to the conclusion that parts of this map were imaginary.

- However, we have a religious feeling about the whole matter. We believe that it was not through any superior wisdom on our part but through the intervention of the God of men and history that we were allowed to discover the truth. There were others who were definitely more worthy than we. It was just that by the kind favor of the Supreme Majesty that THIS was reserved for us to set forth so that we could testify to the fact that there is a God in the universe. When He so wills, He hides. When He so chooses, He reveals. THAT is the answer.

What does the Harris Map prove?

- It shows that there really was a land or continent of Fu Sang, and that land was America; Chinese were there long before Columbus.

- It shows that Hui Shan's "Land of the Women" really existed and that his story of visiting this country is certainly true.

- It places the people of Moderation and Tolerance in the Mogollon region of Arizona right next to the Land of Women, proving the likelihood of the Snake clan as the husbands of the Women.

- It verifies the *Shan Hai Jing* account and proves many Indian tribes of the West were, largely, if not entirely, of Chinese extraction.

- It places the Grand Canyon at the right point and proves that there was extensive contact at a very early time between it and the Far East.

- It identifies the plateau at Mexico City with its White Lake and Depending on Heaven mountains.

- It proves that the ancient Chinese knew about the Gulf of California.

A 1921 California history book records:

> It seems clear that the Chinese had some sort of opportunity to acquire a footing on this (California) coast at least a thousand years before the discovery of America by Columbus.... There are numerous evidences that Chinese or other Orientals visited this coast centuries before the Europeans came.[3]

The back side of the Harris Map Book 5.
Photo taken at the Library of Congress.

**Mr. and Mrs. Hendon Harris III, Dr. Hebert,
Chief of Geography and Maps at the Library of
Congress, and Charlotte Rees.
One of the Harris maps is in the foreground.**

**Hendon Harris III at the Library of Congress with
some of the Dr. Hendon M. Harris, Jr. maps.
Photos taken in 2003.**

CHAPTER 5

The Significance of the Harris "Everything Under Heaven" Maps

[Editor's Note: By the time of Father's death he owned seven similar Asian map books of varying ages and had located twenty-three others of this style. (See text box at end of this chapter). Since then, even more have surfaced. The oldest of Father's maps are late Ming Dynasty. Father believed that all these maps descended from the "mother map" that originally accompanied the *Shan Hai Jing*. The *History of Cartography* states that 72 percent of the place names on this style map are from the *Shan Hai Jing* but that it is unknown when the map originated.]

Understanding the Chinese-Korean world map

Some are perplexed at the age of the ancient Korean and Chinese maps, and I believe this puzzlement is justifiable. One sees certain very archaic things on the maps. Then he sees other things of the sixth century era, and things that he might suspect later. What is the answer?

- The original format or source of the maps was the royal world-survey party of Emperor Yao, under the direction of Prince Yu and Prince Y approximately 2250 B.C.

- Some precious maps evidently survived the Chinese book burnings. The maps were faithfully copied by the Chinese. The Koreans carried on the tradition of faithful map-copying, even *after* their Chinese teachers lost interest in them.

- All the Korean-Chinese world maps go back to one original map. That is why they are so similar. This original map we call the *Shan Hai Jing* mother map.

- It is highly likely that in the fifth century A.D. Buddhists ... beginning with Fa Hien, began to use the maps as the basis of their own histories, and added their own notes and minor changes to them.

- It seems very possible, in fact almost certain, that Hui Shan's group in 458 A.D., on their missionary trip to Fu Sang, took one of the *Shan*

Hai Jing maps to guide them. It was this map that gave them sufficient confidence to believe that they might survive the "America" trip. The route that the five took was by all means the most intelligent. Even in our day it cannot be surpassed for speed and good travel, and the fastest planes from Tokyo to Seattle fly above this sea route ... since it is best for them also.

- In Fu Sang, the Hui Shan party was able to operate with speed and accuracy because they found the Prince Yu map basically correct. It would give them great respect as prophets and seers to tell the various tribes that they knew all about them from the *Shan Hai Jing* and from the old map. No wonder they were so well received.

- Hui Shan was probably tempted to bring his map up to date and may have altered it. He probably did alter it to fit the changes that had taken place in 2600 years. It is very likely that the Koreans used his modified or corrected map in their subsequent copies. This is probably why the sixth century alteration is so apparent.

- Some map copies were poorly or ignorantly done. The British Museum copy has a lot of errors that are the result of copyist ignorance or carelessness—such as calling Annam the Land of the "Southern Males" instead of the "Southern Peace," and miswriting "Rainbow, Rainbow" into something entirely different, and saying the Oregon Giants were twenty-five feet high when the original said thirty-five feet.

- Some maps were purposely twisted a bit, or redesigned. These, of course, lose most of their value. The Harris Fu Sang map is much better than the British Museum one because it is not only earlier but more faithful to the prototype, or original autograph map which I call the "*Shan Hai Jing* Mother Map."

Others in the past came close to the truth about the Small Chinese Maps of Fu Sang

"The existence of Fu Sang is proved beyond question by old Chinese and Japanese maps."[1] It is good to have the statement below of De Paravey, who lived in the nineteenth century, as to the small ancient Chinese maps.

All the maps, rough, and purposely altered as to size of foreign countries, that we have been able to find in the books or collections relating to China, and anterior to date to the exact maps of the

Celestial Empire, which were finally made by the aid of the corrections of the missionaries at Peking, show, in fact, to the east and northeast of China, beyond Japan, marked under one of its names, Ji pen ("Origin of the Sun"), a confused mass of countries, delineated as small islands, undoubtedly because they were reached by sea.[2]

Among these countries of which the size is purposely reduced, is marked the celebrated country of Fu Sang, a country, of which many fables have been related in China, but which in the account translated by M. de Guignes, is presented in a light so entirely natural that it cannot be considered otherwise than as one of the countries of America, even if it is not, as we think possible, intended for the entire Continent of America.

We had not known of the old Chinese maps, drawn up so as to present Europe and all of Asia, outside of China, as very small countries, until our visit to Oxford in 1830. We then copied them at the Bodleian Library, and our scholarly friend, Sir George Stanton, afterward gave us one of these imperfect maps.

Upon returning to London, we there sought and found the Chinese text of the account translated by M. de Guignes; for the works in which it is found are monopolized at Paris by certain students of Chinese. We copied this text, and showed it to Mr. Huttman, then secretary of the English Asiatic Society. He recognized in it, as we did, a description of America, or of one of its parts, and in the surprise which he felt, he communicated, probably, with M. Klaproth regarding our researches, for we were at London again when this Prussian scholar published, in the "Nouvelles Annales des Voyages," in the year 1831 a pretended refutation of the memoirs of M. de Guignes, a refutation which we may some day publish.

Neither this letter nor this printed article changed our convictions as to the justice of the views of the learned M. de Guignes. We declared them to M. Klaproth, and, as he himself undoubtedly felt the feebleness of the arguments by which he had endeavored to prove that this account of Fu Sang should be understood to refer to Japan, he afterward, on this account, as we suppose, wishing to convert M. van Humboldt to his false ideas, caused the insertion, in Vol. X of the "Nouveau Journal Asiatique de Paris," of the letters of the late Pere Gaubil, in which this learned missionary, without disputing this story, discusses the ideas of M. de Guignes, and not knowing anything then of the maps of which we have spoken appears to be unwilling to admit that America under the name of Fu Sang, or under any other name, had been really known to the Buddhists or shamans of High Asia since the year 458 A.D.[3]

De Paravey could have crushed his adversaries with irrefutable proofs... had he gone a bit further, or known a bit more Chinese.

Professor Nakamura had a map at Seoul 34x33 cm, which had all the Fu Sang countries, and yet which has latitude and longitude grid marks, plus the north and south poles designated as such. It is possible that this map goes back to remote antiquity in all its parts and is a proof of Professor Hapgood's contention that the ancient Chinese knew latitude and longitude.

Joseph Needham says:

> Phei Hsiu (224 - 271 A.D.) started the system of grids in which the side of each square represented a stated number of li (approximately half kilometer), which was continued by such eminent geographers as Chia Tan of the Tang (730 - 805 A.D.) and culminated in the magnificent stone-engraved maps of 1137 A.D., which are still in the Oei Lin museum at Xian. The Chinese had, of course, their own distortion, since their orthogonal mesh-net projection did not allow for the curvature of the earth, but the fact remains that between the time of Ptolemy and the Renaissance, the cartography of China was at an immeasurably higher level than that of Europe.[4]

The map which we have mentioned has grid marks that show the curvature of the earth and the north and south poles plus all the countries of Fu Sang. The Paris Chinese map seems to indicate in its notations that the earth is 84,000 li in each direction ... which is almost exactly correct.

Imagine the DARING of showing "Everything Under Heaven." Now we know this cartography was not all imaginary, but mostly real. It was the result of courageous and thorough expedition and survey work.

One gets the impression that to the north Emperor Yao's cartographers made the complete circuit of Lake Baikal. They went east across Siberia and met several tribes. The western expedition got as far as India, and took down descriptions from the people of the sub-continent regarding other nations to the west. To the south they found Siam, Annam, and Malaysia.

The eastern expedition was the most thorough. Range after range was surveyed. The dauntless engineers appointed men to pace off distances in all directions. Central and South America were at least located ... and tribes were fathered. From Alaska to northern Chili the faces of the Chinese were known and their own children took control of several vital areas.

We feel no hesitancy, now that the copies of Yu's maps have been partially interpreted in pronouncing the Chinese the most accurate and brilliant of all ancient cartographers. Four thousand years ago they mapped western North and South America and much of the world. We know that much of this map-making was reasonable and amazingly accurate.

The reason the Chinese and Koreans preserved and copied the ancient maps was because, with true instinct, they believed they were basically correct.

The French map of Fu Sang

In 1737 A.D. the French geographer Philippe Buache, who was an honored member of the Academy, presented it an amazing map. On the Pacific seaboard the coast of what was later to be the Western United States was properly drawn, with California and the Gulf of Baja in place. The American Northwest was shown, and above this was an area where parts of several Canadian provinces now stand ... denominated "FOU SANG."[5]

There is no question in my mind that the great Buache was able to properly denominate the district (or rather, one part of Fu Sang because he had maps ... authentic maps, similar to our Fu Sang Map which showed him the correct ancient name of the district. Buache had proofs of the existence of Fu Sang.

The Paris Chinese map seems to indicate in its notations that the earth is 84,000 li in each direction ... which is almost exactly correct. The "French" Chinese map teaches us the diameter of the big, little and middle-sized stars as 100, 40, and 80 li respectively. The moon and sun are each 5000 li across. The delightful information in no way blemishes the charm and sincerity of their almost desperate effort to be scientifically helpful.

English map shows Fu Sang

In 1768 Thomas Jeffereys, a cartographer of King George the Third, also drew a map[6] which clearly and plainly shows the American Fu Sang. How would this eminent Englishman dare to present the king such a map, unless he had proofs that were unshakeable to his mind?

However, these French and English experts were quietly shoved aside, even though right. The Strait of Anian was "rediscovered" and named the Bering Strait … because the Czar willed it. Dah Han would finally end up as Alaska … through sheer ignorance and crude force.

Comments of Professor Hiroshi Nakamura on old Chinese world maps preserved by the Koreans

Nakamura made a tremendous contribution toward history by his thorough researches in many areas. Nakamura said:

> In old Korea, geographical atlases in the form of ordinary books, stitched with leather, were comparatively rare, but in another form, mounted on screens, were in everyday use. Such an atlas was certainly very convenient, yet it was not commonly found amongst either the Chinese or the Japanese.

> The most surprising thing about these old Korean atlases is that except for very modern examples of the nineteenth century, which show how very completely foreign knowledge had at last invaded the country, they contain invariably the same material, as if they were indifferent to the progress of geographical knowledge. They contain usually the following maps, and in the order given: mappemonde [world map], China, Japan, Liu-Kiu, Korea and the eight provinces of Korea, one map to each province. Occasionally, however, the order is slightly modified, Japan and the Liu-Kiu, or the mappemonde, being put at the end of the atlas. These atlases have survived from ancient times, either as woodcuts or as manuscripts. They reveal very great differences in size, in technical skill displayed, in color and even in title, but none in the content.[7]

I find Professor Nakamura's remarks both interesting and slightly amusing. He describes those very characteristics of the Chinese and Koreans which have enabled them to preserve their way of life despite the ravages of time and of other cultures. The Chinese and Koreans knew how to hang on to the desirable things of the past. However, the Japanese have been quick, in the last hundred years, to adopt new things and methods. The conservatism of old China and old Korea was also a splendid thing. Personally, I am very happy that they refused to change the format of these old maps. They have thereby kept precious ancient geographical facts intact. I will even venture to say that because they refused to surrender the format of their old maps we can now prove that the Chinese discovered America, were the ancestors of several Indian tribes, and that the East Indians, Chinese, Japanese and Koreans were the true builders of the Mexican, Central American, and Peruvian civilizations a thousand years before Columbus dreamed of the new world.

Nakamura quotes memoirs of Yi Ik-Seup:[8] "The Korean mappemondes existed from time immemorial." Nakamura scoffs at the work of Yi, and says it is not worthy of serious criticism, because Yi endeavored to identify topographical names by the literal translation of the Chinese characters, with names in use today. But we wish to defend Yi for at least having tried to interpret the maps. The amazing failure of scholars before us was due to lack of faith and narrowness of trust. Because I believed that Chinese and Korean hands … which had long turned to dust … were honest and faithful hands … I was able to unlock secrets that much wiser men than I were not able to discover. There has been too much scorn and too little research.

were not willing to relegate the *Shan Hai Jing* to the area s, we have been able to fulfill Henriette Mertz's prophecy *n Hai Jing* would eventually prove the greatest travel and l document in history. Yet we would not have known of Yi fessor Nakamura's diligence, and we owe him a true debt for Yi.

e had found an ancient Korean map that contains even Europe a. I am sure he was right, whether Professor Nakamura takes maps seriously or not. Nakamura is particularly offended that one place that the mappemonde dates from time immemorial, er he is trying to identify America in the "ring continent."[9] Yi both counts! The ring continent does include America, and he original maps must exceed four millenniums!

ays:

rean mappemonde has no value whatever from the hical point of view, though it has a certain interest from that of folklore, for all place-names recorded in one or another example, and found here and there in Chinese literature, will one day be identified.

Prof. Nakamura evidently believed that most of the names on the world map are fictitious and fantastic, or "legendary" names from the *Shan Hai Jing*.[10] His opinion is partly justified when we look at the European side of the maps. There we find "Floating Ghosts Country" and some unlikely names. I believe that the misunderstood parts on the left side of these maps caused the students of these maps to come to the conclusion, as does the professor, that he was dealing with little more than speculative nonsense.[11]

As I studied the right side of the maps I was astounded at how true many of the designations were, and how well they matched the statements in the Southern History (Nan Shih) of the Chinese, and exactly maintained the statements in the *Shan Hai Jing*. I was also deeply impressed at the wonderful way they matched both the statements of Hui Shan and the actualities of early American geography, and pre-Columbian history.

Nakamura's vast faith that the Korean maps COULD NOT contain geographical knowledge or instruction is remarkable. Nakamura KNOWS that there is no geographical knowledge in the maps. This is similar to our KNOWING that no good thing can come out of Seoul or Beijing to instruct us in the geography of the past. So, all the Chinese and the Koreans were evidently blind, and drew useless maps which they faithfully preserved because they believed the geography of the ancient world ought to be preserved! Everything in the maps has a LITERARY MEANING, which the professor has not discovered, but ALL of which will be revealed in due time! His is truly a wonderful faith.

We show that the *Shan Hai Jing*, and its maps, and history, especially the parts about "America," form a perfect mutual witness. Forgery, fraud, and error are almost impossible. Everything agrees. The *Shan Hai Jing* is a masterpiece of geography and history… a record of ancient and glorious deeds that now must be known and honored.

Nakamura tells us:

> Now the *Chan Hai King*, with the exception of the first five chapters, originally had accompanying pictures, and the text existed only to explain them. The original pictures were lost in a far-distant

age, and those we see today, representing fantastic monsters, were remade in the 6th century in accordance with the ancient text. Many have therefore believed that the Korean mappemonde, or another very like it, must have been part of the *Chan Hai King*.[12] … we may admit that the *Chan Hai King* could have had a mappemonde as an explanatory picture of its cosmography. Any supposition is feasible, but without solid foundation it remains only supposition. This hypothesis, that the Korean mappemonde had its origin in the *Chan Hai King*, must be admitted only with the greatest reserve. It may be very old, but it need not be as old as that. It cannot have taken on its peculiar form, nor have been given its traditional content, before the 11th century. None of my researches allow me to fix its date earlier than the 16th century. Most of the examples are of the 17th and 18th centuries. On the other hand, the closest examination of its content will not allow me to put its date any later than the 11th century. To soften this contradiction appropriate material must be found to bridge the gap between these two epochs. Such material will come, it is to be hoped, from Chinese sources rather than Korean for this mappemonde is purely Chinese. It bears no trace of anything Korean, which is understandable when we consider the sciences and the arts of Korea were almost always slavishly modeled upon those of China.

Nakamura was wandering close to a great discovery, but he could not believe … could not have faith.[13] (It was inevitable that the mappemonde picked up some later words or interpolations on their long journey out of the past). I do not agree with some of the conclusions of Professor Nakamura. It is my opinion that he has made a serious error by not taking the Chinese book the *Shan Hai Jing* seriously. Yet he cannot be greatly blamed for it has been the habit and tendency of Asiatic scholars for the last two thousand years to belittle the *Shan Hai Jing* through misinterpretation.

Nonetheless, I confess humility before the scholarship of so skilled and deep an interpreter of Asiatic history, and it is only because scientific truth demands that elements which the profound Japanese scholar has not been aware of, be now stressed, that I dare differ with him at all. In fact, it is my belief that if I had had the privilege of meeting this great man, that we would have come to a common understanding.

We are greatly indebted to the professor for giving us a list of many Korean maps of the world … so that our map does not have to stand as an orphan, as it were. It has many brothers and sisters in the world who stand ready to lend their testimony concerning the things which we have discovered, or correlated, and which we now present.

We are particularly happy that Japanese previously delved into these matters … so we do not have to rest our case on European opinions alone. In fact, it is really inappropriate that heretofore we have depended on blind people, as it were, to discuss Oriental matters. We foreigners, so weak in our knowledge of Chinese words, must seem insufferably presumptuous to our Asiatic friends when we make decisions about the Orient without their guidance and help.

But the time for doubts and contradictions is at an end. THERE ARE FOUR THINGS WHICH AGREE:

- THE *SHAN HAI JING*
- THE KOREAN MAPS
- ANCIENT AMERICAN HISTORY
- THE BASIC GEOGRAPHY OF ANCIENT AMERICA

ALL THE PIECES FALL NICELY INTO PLACE.

Nakamura admits: "Even as far back as the Tcheou [Chou] Dynasty, Chinese Cartography was well established, and the court then had regular officials whose duties were concerned with the production and preservation of maps."[14] (To accept the Chou Dynasty date of Nakamura puts us back approximately 2800 years. All that we ask of our readers is to accept another 1300 years, which places us in the time of Minister Yu.)

"Everything Under Heaven" Maps
that Hendon M. Harris, Jr. was aware of [15]

1-7 The Seven Harris Korean map books—each containing seven military maps of old Korea, a map of Japan and the world map

8 The map of the ancient world in the British Museum with several supporting maps in a book

9 Tchien-ha-Tchong-do (Mappemonde), anonymous, no place of publication

10 Mappemonde, anonymous, no place of publication, undated, Mr. Leo Bagrow's collection

11 Nakamura collection. Mappemonde without title, anonymous, no place of publication, undated

12 Mappemonde, Cho-sens-chi-do, Map of Korea, anonymous, no place of publication, undated. Library of the Imperial University of Keijo, Ancient 4709/38

13 Tchien-ha-tchong-do, or Tchien-ha-do (Mappemonde), anonymous, no place of publication, undated. Ecole des Langues Orientales Vivantes, Paris, D. 7989

14 Chio-do-bo (Map Treasures) anonymous, no place of publication, undated, Mr. Hidetaka Nakamura's collection

15 Mappemonde without title, anonymous, no place of publication, undated, Hiroshi Nakamura's collection

16 Mappemonde with total of 13 maps, Hiroshi Nakamura's collection, without title, anonymous, no place of publication, undated

17 Yi-chi-do (Geographical Atlas), by Kum-ho-san-in (Ai-Kieng-chai), no place of publication, zodiacal date–year of the old earth and of the cock. Library of Baron Mitsui

18 Hiroshi Nakamura's collection No. 614, Library of the Imperial University of Keiyo, Ancient 4709/58

19 Ye-chi-do (Geographical Atlas). By Kum-ho-san-in (Lo-on-gun at Honan), ancient … Prof T. Okudaera's collection

20 Tong-kuk-ye-chi-do (Korean Atlas-title printed on cover. Prof. Hiroshi Nakamura

21 Chi-do-pien (Geographical Atlas-MS. title), by Lo-on-gun at Honan. Prof. H. Nakamura

22 Chi-do (Geographical Maps), anonymous, no place of publication, undated. Prof. H. Nakamura's collection No. 417

23 Chi-Kwal (Summary of Geography), anonymous, no place of publication, undated. Prof. H. Nakamura's collection No. 609

24 Ye-chi-do (Geographical Atlas), anonymous, no place of publication, undated. Library of the Imperial University of Keijo, Ancient 4709/37.

25 Chi-do (Geographical Maps), anonymous, no place of publication, undated. Prof. H. Nakamura's collection No. 414 Fig. 3

26 Without title, anonymous, no place of publication, undated. Prof. H. Nakamura's collection No. 1321

27 Ye-chi-do (Geographical Atlas) anonymous, no place of compilation, undated. Library of His Highness Prince Yi, Historical Division, Geographical Section, No. 42 (Fig. 4)

28 Ye-do (Geographical Atlas), anonymous, no place of compilation, undated. Museum of the Central Government of Korea

29 Chi-do (Geographical Maps), anonymous, no place of compilation, undated. Museum of the Central Government of Korea, Cho, 61/27

It is certain that there are several more copies of the ancient *Shan Hai Jing* Map in existence. The passage of time and ravages of war have probably already scattered some of the maps mentioned above.

Harris Map Collection being studied at the Library of Congress.
In photo from left to right are Dr. Hwa-Wei Lee, Chief, Asian Division,
the Library of Congress, Charlotte Rees, Dr. Xiaocong Li, Professor of
Historical Geography and Cartography, Peking University, Beijing.

CHAPTER 6
Chinese Map Making

Chinese geography and its influences

The Chinese language is full of geographical symbols of great antiquity. Vining pointed out that the character for river (chuan) is an ancient graph of flowing water. The word for field (tien) shows enclosed and divided space. The character for mountain (shan) was once an actual drawing of a mountain with three peaks.[1] Here we have proof, in the Chinese language itself, which goes back to very early eras, that the Chinese, masters of the pictographic, have been drawing maps of one kind or another since time immemorial.

One of the oldest Chinese geographic documents is the *Yu Gung (Tribute of Yu)* chapter of the *Shu Jing (Historical Classic)* which Professor Needham places five centuries before Christ. However, we believe it almost contemporary with Emperor Yu, and dates approximately 2200 B.C.

In the *Tribute of Yu* mentioned above, the nine provinces are listed. Their soils, products, and waterways are discussed. It constitutes an early economic geography. It is a fact, hard for Westerners to accept, but from all evidences the Chinese were making good maps, some 2500 years before we were.

In the Former Han period [202 B.C. - A.D. 9] the Director General of the Masses Ta Ssu Tu had the function of preparing maps of the feudal principalities. Directors of Regions (Chih Fan Shih) were placed in charge of the maps of the empire. The Geographer-Royal (Thu Hsun) took care of the maps of provincial circuits. When the Emperor was making a tour of inspection he rode close to the imperial vehicle in order to explain the characteristics of the country and its products.[2]

When Chin Shih Huang became emperor, he burned everybody's books but kept the maps, assembling them from all over the empire. He felt books might ruin the thoughts of the people but maps had no political ideas.

When Chang Chien returned from the West (126 B.C.), the emperor consulted ancient maps and books and decided that the mountain from which the Yellow River took its source should be called Kun-lun.[3]

In 116 A.D. Chang Heng occupied himself with map making and he presented a Ti Hsing Thu. This great genius originated the rectangular grid system ... if reports were correct. He cast a network of coordinates about heaven and earth and reckoned on the basis of it.

Chinese women also did some remarkable things in the field of map making. In the late third century A.D., Wang Chia in his *Memoirs of Neglected Matters* tells us: "(Emperor) Sun Chuan (reigned 222 A.D. to 248 A.D. as the first emperor to the Wu State) searched for an expert painter to draw a map, with mountains, rivers, and all physical features, for military purposes. The younger sister of the prime minister was presented [as a suitable person], and he asked her to [draw] the mountains, rivers, and lakes of the nine areas.[4] She suggested that as the colors of a drawing would fade, it would be better to make the map in embroidery, and this was accordingly done ..."

Pei Hsiu, who was Minister of Works in 267 A.D., was called by some the father of scientific cartography in China. "The 35th chapter of the *Chin Shu* preserves particulars of map making in which he then engaged, together with the text of his preface to the maps."[5]

This is what Pei Hsiu said:

> Now referring back to antiquity, I have examined according to the *Yu Gung* the mountains and lakes, the courses of the rivers, the plateaus and plains, the slopes and marshes, the limits of the nine ancient provinces and the sixteen modern ones, taking account of commanderies and fiefs, prefectures and cities, and not forgetting the names of places where the ancient kingdoms concluded treaties or held meetings, and lastly, inserting the roads, paths, and navigable waters, I have made this map in eighteen sheets.[6]

In making a map there are six principles observable:

1. The graduated divisions which are the means of determining the scale of which the map is to be drawn.

2. The rectangular grid (of parallel lines in two dimensions), which is the way of depicting the correct relations between the various parts of the map.

3. Pacing out the sides of right-angled triangles, which is the way of fixing the lengths of derived distances (i.e. the third side of the triangle which cannot be walked over).

4. (Measuring) the high and the low.

5. (Measuring) right angles and acute angles.

6. (Measuring) curves and straight lines. These three principles are used according to the nature of the terrain, and are the means by which one reduces what are really plains and hills (lit. cliffs) to distances on a plane surface.

If one draws a map without having graduated divisions, there is no means of distinguishing between what is near and what is far. If one has graduated divisions, but no map, one will certainly lose it elsewhere (i.e., in the middle, far from guiding marks). If one has a rectangular grid, but has not worked upon the tao li principle, then when it is a case of places in difficult country, among mountains, lakes or seas (which cannot be traversed directly by the surveyor), one cannot ascertain how they are related to one another. If one has adopted the tao li principle, but has not taken account of the high and low, the right angles and acute angles, and the curves and straight lines, then the figures for distances indicated on the paths and roads will be far from the truth, and will lose the accuracy of the rectangular grid.[7]

Pei Hsiu left us this remarkable statement, which proves the abilities of Chinese map makers by 267 A.D. It is our belief that many of the principles he mentions are not original with him, but go back to distant antiquity. In any event, we know that the rectangular grid was at least as old as Pei Hsiu … and probably had been used since the day of Emperor Yao.

The ancient custom of Buddhist map making

Chinese pilgrims and missionaries in the early days often made maps and wrote descriptions of their travels. Charles Leland tells us, "On account of the great distance to the Land of Fu Sang, no missionaries went there afterwards." Yet the story of this land, so full of marvels, has not yet disappeared from the memories of Chinese and Buddhist enquirers into the wonders of the olden times. "Many of them have frequently mentioned it in their works, and have even drawn maps of it ..."[8]

It was a common practice among the early Buddhist missionaries of India and China to write descriptions of their travels, and they would draw maps of the places they had been. The celebrated scholar Stanislas Julien has versions of Buddhist travels in the French language, which fill over 1500 octavo pages, in his collections. It is evident that it was a special matter of pride among Buddhist missionaries to excel their predecessors in the extent of their journeys and in the zeal of success with which they distributed the doctrines and sacred images of Buddha.

Julien says,

> From the fourth century of the Christian era to the tenth, the Chinese pilgrims who went into the countries west of China ... have published a great number of narratives, itineraries, and descriptions, more or less extended, of the countries which they visited. Unfortunately the greater part has perished, unless they remain buried in some obscure convent in China. Thus we cannot sufficiently regret the loss of the description of Western countries by Chi-Tao-An, a Chinese shaman who became a monk in 316 A.D. and consequently preceded Fa-Hien, who did not go forth until 339 A.D. The loss most to be regretted is unquestionably *The Description of Western Countries* in sixty volumes with four books of pictures and maps which, edited in accordance with an Imperial decree by many official writers after the memoirs of the most distinguished religious and secular authors, appeared in the year 666, with an introduction written by the Emperor Kao-Thsang, the cost being defrayed by the government.

It would take too much time to tell of the six works which are to be found in France and Russia on the subject of Buddhist travels. First is the memoirs of the *Kingdom of Buddha*, by Fa-Hien, a Chinese monk who lived in 399 A.D. and visited 30 kingdoms. Second, the *Memoirs of Hoei-Seng and Song-Yun*, envoys to India in 518 by order of the Empress. Third, *Memoirs of Western Countries*, edited in 648 by Hiouen-Thsang. Fourth, *History of the Convent of Grand Benevolence.* Fifth, *The History and Journey of Fifty-six Monks in the Tang Dynasty.* Sixth is the *Itinerary of the Travels of Khi-Nie.*[9]

Probably these also had map illustrations.

Now that we have seen there were maps made by Buddhist missionaries, we can more readily accept the fact that the monk Hui-Shan had a map of his travels. (It is very likely that the Harris Fu Sang Map is a copy of the Hui Shan revision of the *Shan Hai Jing* Map.) We believe he prepared it after his trip to Fu Sang and left it with the Koreans to explain America and his trip there. They faithfully copied it and preserved it. We can also regard the *Book of the Mountains and the Seas (Shan Hai Jing)* written by the Chinese millennia earlier to be essentially true. It says, "Go so many li and you will see such and such a thing." The Harris Map vindicates it.

Early European maps of America borrowed from somewhere

Anian is Dah Han

As early as 1531 Englishmen had begun to erect vast schemes of new world expansion. About that time Robert Thorne and Roger Barlow composed the *Declaration of the Indies*, in which they urged a voyage northwards from England over the Pole and then south through the Strait of Anian, which, as one author said, was the "The undiscovered passage supposed to divide America from Asia."[10] But the Strait of Anian, and Anian itself, DID exist. Just because Bering later rediscovered it and had it named after himself still doesn't answer the question how the English had known such a strait existed in the year 1531. The English could not have known about the Strait of Anian unless somebody had gone to Dah Han and seen it. The fact that it was discovered exactly where Thorne and Barlow thought it would be proves that Dah Han and the Strait of Dah Han were not Chinese pipe-dreams, but were real places.

At Huntington Library in the fall of 1972 we found a map of America drawn by H. Mosting in the eighteenth century which shows the Kingdom of Anian to the northwest of the Strait of Anian, that is on the Asiatic side, but it also has Anian on the American side and shows California as an island.

In 1901 E. H. Parker published a book, which is in the Archives of the Huntington Library, named *China, Her History, Diplomacy and Commerce*. Opposite page 128 is a map of northern China twice marked "totally unknown to Chinese at all times." Both Siberia and Anian are so designated. We hope the Chinese will take this "fact" to heart and henceforth deny they have ever been in Anian which is Dah Han, and which was evidently discovered by the Chinese in the first place!

Zalteri in 1566 placed the Strait of Anian between Asia and America.[11] Mercator in 1569 so placed it also and has Anian Regnum on the Alaska side (Kingdom of Anian).[12] This is Dah Han, which is indicated on the Harris Fu Sang Map.

The Darien error

Robert Thorne's Spanish Map of the World[13] (1527) shows South America in a shape almost exactly as the real shape of North America. It has a place called Darien, almost exactly in proportion to the place where the Harris Fu Sang Map shows Dah Ren. His actual North America has no West Coast.

We strongly suspect that the early Spanish and English cosmographers had an Arab or Chinese Map as a parallel source, and misplaced Darien through sheer ignorance of the location and the material they were dealing with. Further confirmation of this is their resorting to the medieval device of letting the map of North America run out of space on the left, so avoiding an unfamiliar area. At the point where Thorne put Darien is a close similarity of the Central American narrow ribbon of land to the contour of the Aleutians in its relationship to Alaska. Darien was named after Dah Ren. Dah Ren is Alaska.

Cartography and the Pacific Coast of America

There is in existence a very remarkable Turkish Map made in the year 1513. The Eastern hemisphere on this map appears to be rather ordinary. However, as Professor Hapgood points out, "If this is true of the Eastern hemisphere it is an entirely different story in the West…it is evident that the cartographer had at his disposal some most extraordinary source material. The shapes of North and South America have a surprisingly modern look. The western coasts are exceptionally interesting. They seem to be about two centuries ahead of the cartography of the time. Furthermore, they appear to have been drawn on the highly sophisticated spherical projection. The shape of what is now the United States is about perfect."[14]

Hapgood speaks of the remarkable accuracy of the Pacific Coast of the Americas and the difficulty in imagining how these maps could be drawn in the middle of the sixteenth century. Yet, during the sixteenth century maps actually deteriorated in correctness, because they failed to depend on the ancient source drawings.

Professor Hapgood made a study of a famous map of China that had
been carved in stone, in China, in the year 1137 A.D. Although the map
was carved in that year it is known to have been in existence for an
indefinite period before that. It contains a wonderful representation of the
river systems of China. After carefully studying this map, Dr. Hapgood
and his students realized that the square grid found on that map was
something that had been superimposed on the map by men ignorant of
its original true projection. In other words, what revealed itself here was
the oblong grid found on the Peri Reis Map, noted on the Ptolemy Maps,
and found, through spherical trigonometry, on the D'Canerio map. The
Chinese map was discovered based on an advance cartography which
included spherical trigonometry and the use of effective instruments
for determining latitudes and longitudes. In China the square grid
was apparently imposed on the maps by later people who had entirely
forgotten the science by which it was drawn in the days of their early
fathers. Hapgood assures us that we have evidence that when this ancient
map of China was first drawn, map makers of Asia had means of finding
longitude as accurately as they found latitude, exactly as was the case
with the Portolan charts in the West. He assures us that as far as longitude
was concerned the errors both on the East and West balanced out to zero
… and that the average error of latitude was very small.

Hapgood makes this final conclusion:

> It seems to me that the evidence of this, the Chinese Map, points
> to the existence in very ancient times of a world-wide civilization,
> the map makers of which mapped virtually the entire globe with
> a uniform general level of technology, with similar methods,
> equal knowledge of mathematics, and probably the same source
> of instruments. I regard this Chinese map as the capstone of the
> structure I have erected in this book. For me it settles the question
> as to whether the ancient culture that penetrated Antarctica and
> originated all the original western maps was indeed world-wide.[15]

If it is true that the ancient Chinese were well able to find latitude and
longitude, and were as capable as anyone in the world when it came to
navigation, then do not at last the barriers to our belief that Chinese ships
could have sailed to our shores and returned with ease fall down? The
Harris Fu Sang Map and the many other maps prove that the Chinese had
come … to the "American" shores and that the Chinese could make good
and capable ships for the round-trip journey.

Harris Map Collection being studied at the Library of Congress. On the left Dr. Judy Lu, China Area Specialist of the Library of Congress looks on as Young Ki Lee, expert in ancient Korean, studies Korean inscriptions on the maps.

CHAPTER 7

Mysteries of the Grand Canyon

For thousands of years the Chinese knew of Fu Sang and the place there they dreamed of most was that glorious series of subterranean mountains and temples known now as the Grand Canyon of the Colorado.

The Womb and the Navel of the Earth

From Chinese sources and from Indian traditions it appears that the terms Womb of the Earth and Navel of the Earth were connected with the Grand Canyon. The sun and the Grand Canyon seem points of reference for astronomical determination to indicate deviations. Since mathematics requires more than one point of reference, it seems necessary that we study the significance of these two points that are definitely named.

The Grand Canyon is the chief place of Fu Sang. It is the Master Key to the whole picture of Chinese prowess on our continent.

George Horton James has given a very graphic record of his extensive travels and researches in the Grand Canyon area.[1] He gives a description of the Colorado River gliding somberly through the Canyon of Desolation with everything dreary and forsaken. Next, the river passes Lighthouse Rock, Glen Canyon and Marble Canyon with their rapids and dangers. Afterwards appear the granite gorges of the Grand Canyon, places of deepest gloom, where the sun never touches the water. Here are great waterfalls and deep cuts through black and forbidding lava, but the water flows on. It enters Black Canyon, finally emerging into open peaceful slopes of the desert, and then on down to the Gulf of California.

It is most remarkable that the ancient kings of China also had a place in Fu Sang called the Somber Residence and the Valley of Obscurity or Desolation, where they sent their astronomers to make astronomical observations. In the *Shu King* we have noticed that Emperor Yao sent astronomers to the Valley of Obscurity and the Somber Residence "to observe the movements of the Sun and the Moon and the Syzygies, or the orbital points of the conjunctions. Also to investigate and inform the people of the order of the seasons."[2] It is also said that Yao introduced a calendar reform bringing the seasons into accord with the observations. He did the same with the months and corrected the days.

In the Yu Kuei report of Hui Shan's trip to Fu Sang in the fifth century, the Black Canyon is mentioned. I believe that this Black Canyon is the very canyon, along with the main portion of what is known as the Grand Canyon, which was the observatory area for the ancients.

Indian legends about the Grand Canyon area

According to George W. James, the Paiuti Tribe believes that the gods from above will return to the earth, and Angel Gate is to be their place of descent. These gods will return and lead them to more beautiful, fertile, and better-watered lands, where seeds, fruits, flowers, and vegetables will abound. (These Paiuti are probably the "White People" of the *Shan Hai Jing* Record. Pai in Chinese is "white.") I believe this is a reference to the old Asian astronomers and spiritual guides who did lead a great number of the early inhabitants to Maya land. It has been the duty of certain Grand Canyon area shamans or medicine men on given days of the year to watch for the return of these ancient men. So the Indians call it The Gateway of the People of the Shadows, and the priests sit where they can watch Angel Gate from rising to setting of the sun that they may be ready to warn their people when those from above come to lead them to their blessed homes of plenty, comfort and rest.[3]

This whole area is a sacred place to the Indians. James himself said "to me this canyon is the Holy of the Holies, the inner temple where each man may be his own high priest and stand face to face with the Divine."[4] He cited an incident from the old pioneer days when a man named Lieutenant Ives tried to investigate the old Hopi salt trail from Oraibli and received a very mysterious and uncooperative attitude from the Hopi elders. When he had sought in vain to find the salt mines, he returned to his Indian host, who said, "I told you so," and offered to give him a guide to Fort Defiance 150 miles to the East.[5]

We can state with assurance that the Hopi still regard the great chasm with awe and wonder. About a mile from Havasupai point are the remains of what was once, undoubtedly, a circular lookout point built of stone. It is 300 feet in diameter and commands a more extensive view than any other point on the south rim of the canyon for miles around. James says that from this point the higher walls of the north side of the canyon and every prominent landmark east, west, and south are clearly seen including the Navajo Mountains 200 miles away to the northeast, Mt. Trumbull on the northwest and the ranges of California in the west. Numbers of pieces of pottery, of corrugated and other ancient types, are found on the mound in great profusion.

At the head of the Mystic Spring trail are the ruins of a prehistoric house of which the Havasupai know nothing. It was there long before their ancestors were born, and as to how old it is, they have no tradition. It seems highly likely that this place may have been one of the main observation points of olden-times Chinese and East Indians. To this day at the canyon we have Mt. Observation which can be climbed and would be an incomparable observatory.

Another amazing fact is that in the Grand Canyon itself the names are almost entirely Asiatic. We have Shiva Temple, Confucius Temple, and a structure of red-walled limestone so much like the prehistoric temples of Yucatan, that to this day it is called Yucatan Temple.[6] We must not suppose these names accidental. Those who built the Teotihuacan and Yucatan temples and who recruited people from this area for the Mexico and Mayan civilizations no doubt copied this natural structure.

The legend, which is really no legend, of nine suns being shot down at the Place where the Sun was Born, will finally be found to refer to the "sun-shots" of the ancient astronomers, who after the cataclysms and the geological and sidereal disturbances of the post-deluge period, reoriented the times and seasons. Certainly the Grand Canyon Indians verify this with their traditions of the Men from Heaven who reestablished their days for them. The Chinese stories of how Emperors Yao and Yu labored to reestablish the disordered skies and earth, and their scientific expeditions to Fu Sang, all tie together with the ancient maps, Indian tradition, Grand Canyon geography and the records that Confucius preserved.

The fourteenth book of the *Shan Hai Jing* is called the *Classic of the Great Eastern Waste*. Now is it not obvious, looking east from China across the ocean, that the vast deserts of the American west are really the Great Waste in the East as far as Asiatics are concerned? And the first thing that is mentioned in this Waste is the Great Canyon, where a stream flows in a bottomless ravine. There is only one canyon so vast and wonderful that it would be known as that canyon. That it forms a "charming gulf" (the Sea of California) identifies it for certain.

The "Dissipation of Sorrows" calls it Kiang-shang's Great Canyon and it is in Shao-Hao's Country. Shao-Hao's descendant, the Emperor Chwen-suh, left his zither there. We believe this meant that the emperor was so struck by the amazing beauty and loveliness of the canyon that he hung up his musical instrument, so to speak, and never played again.

> Never again on earth, shall this sweet zither,
>> Its gentle songs of China play.
> These mighty depths make proudest music hither,
>> My song shall cease after this glorious day.

We are told that there flows a delightful spring, and those who have visited the lower levels of the canyon know of the Havasupai village and its fine streams and beautiful mountain in the midst of the canyon in all its gorgeous coloration. This was the place where the sun and the moon rose, and, looking eastward along the canyon we see it truly seems so. There is no spot more dramatic in the whole world than this one.

The Canyon

Henriette Mertz says:

> If the fabled country across the "Great Eastern Sea," of which Yu has left descriptive notes, were non-existent, why did so many poets tingle with excitement when they wrote of the spectacular beauty of the "Great Luminous Canyon?" Why did so many poets write, "I saw the place where the sun was born?" Why did others feel that they had been cheated, because they had been born too late and were unable to travel to the place where the sun was born? One poet of the T'ang Dynasty (618 A.D.) regretted that Confucius had traveled extensively in the west but had failed to go east to the place of the sun. The inspiring sight of the "Great Luminous Canyon" thrilled those poetic souls. It could not fail to do so.

> For centuries Chinese scholars had studied this *Book of Mountains and Seas*—this record of Yu. It was one of the required books that all students had to read, and on which they were examined during the time of the great examinations of China.[7]

And it was this book that told such glorious things of the "Low Bright Mountains" of the immense chasm.

Meeting regarding Harris Maps at the Library of Congress. In photo are Gavin Menzies, Dr. John Hebert, Chief Geography and Maps, the Library of Congress, and Charlotte Rees.

CHAPTER 8
Astronomers and Observatories in Fu Sang

"It is in Fu Sang that Hwang-Ti's Astronomers resided who were charged with the observation of the rising sun."[1]

It is significant that Asia's first mentioned contacts with Fu Sang were based on astronomical considerations. Chinese records tell us that the Chinese Emperor sent official agents and court astronomers along with their families to the New World. This was done in order to reset the months, years, and seasons after the great catastrophes of the third millennium B.C. Constant activities of the Indians as star and sun observers were perhaps connected with early Chinese astronomy.

There seem to have been periodic teams of astronomers traveling to Fu Sang to observe movements of the sun and stars. These observations appear both from Chinese reports, traditions, from our maps, and Indians' reports. They were made in and around the Grand Canyon of the Colorado and Black Canyon just beyond.

It might be asked why the astronomers would travel from China to America to make astronomical observations and watch the phases of the moon and movements of the sun. It is well known that only through a comparison of relative movements can the true orbits of the heavenly bodies be correctly determined. The California Coast and the Grand Canyon lie due east of China. It was at a location due east, deep in the matrix of the earth, that a natural observatory, perhaps the most ideal observatory in the world, was situated.

The shadows of the Obscure Valley (Grand Canyon) would make possible a more clearly delineated picture of the heavens, even as it is reported that from a certain passage in the Pyramid of Cheops actions of the Pole Star can be carefully observed. In another location an English astronomer, Herschel, used a three-story chimney flue as a deep telescope and shaft to observe the heavens. The Grand Canyon would provide that place. It was probably necessary that the Chinese go to the Land of Peace, where among the People of Moderation and Tolerance, they could conduct their operations.

I heard from friends of mine that while they were visiting the Hopi at the time of the fall equinox, Hopi elders told them that their observers were out that very night, making the usual astronomical determinations customary at that season. The traditions of the Indians support that the Grand Canyon was an ancient astronomical center.

We know that Hui Shan and the four other Indian shamans were astronomers. I believe it was those five East Indians who revised the calendar. Howard Spinden, curator emeritus of Brooklyn Museum, tells us that the astronomical congress which took place on September 2, 503 A.D. was in order to set the month "Pop" in order. He also states that among the Mayans, astronomy—the understanding of which made possible the calendar—was of first importance.[2]

Possibly those of Hui Shan's four brother priests who were still alive at that time were at this congress. Without their rich knowledge of astronomy the other astronomers would only have been able to do inferior work, if any work at all. It is quite significant that the astronomical society meeting in Copan in 503 A.D. was only one year after Hui made his report to the king of the Liang Dynasty in 502. I consider it a fact of prime importance that these two dates are so close. In the sixth century the entire East Indian calendar system was revised.

A powerful proof of ancient worldwide astronomy

It is well known that it was the astronomers who knew the time and place of the birth of Jesus Christ.[3] From where did this magnificent accuracy of knowledge of astronomy come?

Joseph Needham tells us that the position of Ta Chio (Chinese for Arcturus) in Bootes needs a remark. It has on each side, east and west, two small groups of three stars each. They are called the Shethi or Assistant Conductors by the Chinese. He mentions that a first century B.C. treatise, *The Spring and Autumn Annals* (which he deems apocryphal), describes the actions of the Assistant Conductors. "They lead by the hand Arcturus on one side and the Great Bear on the other, connecting them with what is below."[4]

When I read these astonishing words I immediately remembered the Book of Job. Nearly all scholars, Jewish, Catholic, and Protestant, reckon it to be the oldest record in the Bible. It also contains a wealth of scientific statements, though science is not its primary emphasis. Among the

"Heavenly questions" that Jehovah asked Job, we find this query in Chapter 38:32-33. "Canst thou bring forth Mazzaroth in his season? Or canst thou guide Arcturus with his sons? Knowest thou the [astronomical] ordinances of heaven? Canst thou set the dominion thereof in the earth?" [KJV]

- *The Spring and Autumn Annals* CANNOT be apocryphal if they confirm the Bible in such an amazing way, and at such an early time.

- These statements link ancient Palestine and the mid-east with China. Because they both speak of leading Arcturus and his partner by the hand, or personal guidance, and THEY BOTH CONNECT THESE HEAVENLY ACTIONS WITH WHAT IS BELOW ... we are forced to see that there was an ancient common fund of astronomical knowledge, clearly set forth here.

The world wide linkage of the ancient astronomers cannot be imaginary. Hapgood and others have foreseen this. The world observatories MUST have been a reality, and even as we see the confederacy of master astronomers descending on Jerusalem at the time of Christ's birth, we find their finger in the Book of Job, and in *The Spring and Autumn Annals* of the Chinese.

At Yang-Cheng in Henan (the province where I entered the world) the Chinese had an observatory for more than two thousand years according to Needham.[5]

It is true, as de Saussure points out, that "Greek astronomy was ecliptic, angular, true, and annual while Chinese astronomy was equatorial, horary, mean, and diurnal."[6] However, there were movements of certain stars and constellations observed by both areas.

Herodotus tells us that Thales of Miletus in 585 B.C. predicted an eclipse which actually occurred on May 28 of that year.[7] St. Augustine stated that Thales was able to predict solar and lunar eclipses through his knowledge of astronomical calculations.[8]

Gordon states, "Scientists, by Augustine's time (fourth century A.D.) established the cycle of eclipses through observation ... they must have done so on the basis of global coverage. More precisely, the minimal coverage required for establishing the cycle is at three longitudinal bands 120 degrees apart."[9]

We believe Gordon is right and that his statement amplifies what Charles Hapgood has said about the Chinese ability in the pre-Christian era to determine latitude and longitude and other important matters of science, as early as 4,000 or more years ago. This knowledge was supposedly later lost for many centuries. However, here, global coverage is mentioned!

The Chinese ancient book *Long-Wei-Pi-Shu* cites an opinion of the Buddhist writer Kuan-Mei demonstrating how anciently the knowledge of Fu Sang went back among the Chinese. "It is in Fu Sang that Hwang-Ti's astronomers resided who were charged with the observation of the rising Sun." Hwang-Ti was the first sovereign of the times reputed historical, and first cycle of the Chinese commenced in his reign in the twenty-seventh century B.C."[10] The Chinese attribute invention of the astronomical globe and institution of their cycle system to this great man, Hwang-Ti. I personally see no reason to doubt the Chinese account.

Having spent my boyhood in China, I remember that my father always had great respect for Chinese rumors. On more than one occasion he saved our lives by believing what the Chinese told him was happening. I remember as a child sleeping all night in a Chinese mail sack when we rode a freight train out of Kaifeng after the Chinese had told my father that he had better get us out of the Province of Henan because of strong anti-British sentiments, when students were shot at Shanghai. At Nanking, sure enough, Father actually had to argue for our lives with a mob who wanted to kill us, thinking we were English.

Later, my father left China when the Chinese told him the Japanese were certainly going to attack America. On the day that he was being called a war-monger, he, safely back in America, received the first report of Pearl Harbor. During the Korean War, Chinese Nationalist agents found Communist Chinese were massing troops on the northern frontier at the Yalu River. The Americans did not take them seriously, and we were almost swamped when that great deluge of Chinese human waves came pouring across the frontier, driving us back with the relentless pressure of huge masses of men. Anyone who has dealt with the Chinese and their records knows that you had better listen to a Chinese when he writes or he speaks.

MAP 6

Dr. Hendon M. Harris
Collection

**The cover of this map book has many old
inscriptions on it, adding to its intrigue.**

CHAPTER 9
The Government Commission of Hsi and Ho

According to the Government commission of Hsi and Ho, whom Needham refers to, these were the orders (in part):

> (Hwang-Ti) commanded the (brothers), Hsi and Ho, in reverent accordance with the august heavens, to compute and delineate the sun, moon and stars, and the celestial markers, and so to deliver respectfully the seasons, to be observed by the people.
>
> He particularly ordered the younger brother Hsi to reside among the Yu barbarians (at the place called) Yang-Ku and to receive as a guest the rising sun, in order to regulate the labors of the east (the spring).
>
> He further ordered the youngest brother Hsi to go and live at Nan-Chiao in order to regulate the works of the south and pay respectful attention to the (summer) solstice.
>
> He ordered Ho to reside in the west (at the place called) Nei-Ku, and to bid farewell … to the setting sun.
>
> He further ordered the brother Ho to go and live in the region of the north (at the place called) Yu-Tu, in order to supervise the works of the north.[1]

1. I wish to call attention to the fact that Hsi and Ho are called brothers. Thus, possibly, they are the "Hero Twins" of the Hopi traditions.

2. Notice that Hsi was ordered to stay at Yang Ku among the Yu barbarians. Now this: Yang Ku is nothing else than the short form of chao yang jj ku, which is the Valley of the Manifestation of the Dawn, WHICH IS THE GRAND CANYON. Yu barbarians were the overseas tribes in the New World.

3. I believe it safe to believe from study of the Harris Fu Sang map where the Hsi and Ho country is found in Central America, that the ancient SOUTH Chiao refers to an area south of the Great Valley in Fu Sang.

The Gulf of California and/or Gulf of Mexico was evidently then known as the SOUTH Sea, or a part thereof. Since the area that the brothers were responsible for was so vast, it is no wonder they started new nations not only at the Grand Canyon but in the region of the South as well, that is, below Mexico. We know, also, that when Huan Tow went to the South Sea to worship the spirit of his father he wound up in Yucatan! It seems plain that south to the ancient Chinese often involved places clearly in the southeast! The "ring-continent" delusion would help further the illusion as to where "south" really was.

Rules for Chinese astronomers

The *Shu Ching*, one of the ancient Chinese records, tells us of the very harsh rules for ancient Chinese astronomers. One can only speculate on the mental condition of modern astronomers if the peacefulness of their celestial observations were disturbed by the following federal law, which applied to those luckless persons who engaged in heavenly observations during the earliest Chinese era. "Being before the time, astronomers are to be killed without respite; and being behind the time they are to be slain without reprieve."

This law no doubt greatly aided attention to duty, but there must have been a decline in applicants for the office. In fact, such strict rules effectively destroyed the Astronomical Class itself. As the poets might say, "Time's cruel hand removed them thence, unto a land where time can touch them never more."

I remember when I lived in Taiwan a few years ago, the local government became disturbed by the alarming number of auto accidents, so a law was passed that if a car killed somebody the driver was to be removed from his automobile and shot on the spot. The immediate result was that when a driver killed one person he would often kill several more getting away. The government quickly decided that death has its sting when you give a driver no chance to escape penalties.

Reputedly the astronomers Ho and Hsi were eventually put to death because they had gotten drunk. Therefore the Prince of Yin cut off their heads because he claimed that they had not seen an eclipse that no one else had noticed either. It is undoubtedly true that from this period, in the third millennium B.C., astronomers reported many more eclipses than actually took place, but the quality of astronomers deteriorated.

To give an example of how badly, we submit Shih Ching's report, 776 B.C. as Ionides reports it: "Tenth moon, her conjunction first day Sin-Mao, sun he had an eclipse, also very bad. That moon in eclipse is a thing only common. This sun in eclipse is a thing very bad."[2]

Who were Hsi and Ho?

In actuality Hsi and Ho must have been extraordinary men. The garbled Japanese record is as follows, in its translation of the ancient story: "Beyond the southeastern ocean, between the Kan-shui, or the 'Pleasant Rivers,' is the Kingdom of Hi-ho-koue (or, according to the Japanese pronunciation of the characters, Ghi-wa-kokf). There lived the virgin Hi-ho (Ghi-wa), who espoused Ti-tsiun, and gave birth to ten suns." The same book also says that Hi-ho (Ghi-wa) is the name of a kingdom among the countries of the east, which is also called "The Place Where the Sun Rises."

A passage of the *Shan Hai Jing T'sang-chu*, which is a commentary upon the *Shan Hai Jing*, says "In the days of the Emperor Hwang-Ti, Hi-ho (Ghi-wa) was the astronomer charged with the observations of the sun. This prince having given him the country of Fu Sang, he embarked with his family, settled there and gave this country the name of Hi-ho-koue (Ghi-wa-kokf), or the country of Hi-ho. He had ten children: the boys were named Yen (in Japanese, Fiko), or the male sun; and the girls Ke (in Japanese, Fime), or the female sun: the sun being considered as the source of all fecundity."[3]

Here we have strangely mixed up stories, in which Hi and Ho mean four different things. In the Ionides account there are two Chinese astronomers named Hi and Ho. Then Hi Ho is presented as a virgin girl who married Ti Tsuin the father of nations in Fu Sang. This name is also given to a kingdom in the east. We have the account, which I feel is more probable—Hsi and Ho were the official overseas astronomers for Hwang-Ti, and having journeyed to the new world, fathered the "ten suns" [ten children]. Hsi and Ho must have paved the way for the later journeys of Prince Y and Yu the Great to Fu Sang. These two latter princes went there to control nine suns (sons) that were out of line. It is not impossible that the early Japanese got the suns and the sun-children mixed up.

In any event we have a very clear statement that the Chinese were fathers of the people across the Eastern Ocean. The famous Chinese dictionary *Dz Hai* tells us "The persons Shi and Ho were in charge of the calendar of the Emperor Yao. The *Shan Hai Jing* tells us that the land of Shi-Ho was between the pleasant rivers." The Harris Fu Sang Map shows Hsi and Ho land in the Central America region. Are Hsi and Ho, the Twins of Hopi mythology, who led the people up and out of the dark chasm of ignorance? I am inclined to think so but cannot present the clinching proof.

The Power Shout

It is true that the Hopis give the power shout "Hi Ho" even to our time. There is a probable connection between this and the fact that Hsi and Ho were their first ancestors. It is possible that their original name was Ho-Hsi or people of Ho and Hsi. The Beloved Twins of Hopi folklore were their finest and most respected teachers. It is very likely that the Twins were Ho and Hsi themselves.

CHAPTER 10
Chinese Inventions

Early Chinese compass

It is probably true that the Chinese were the inventors of the compass. According to their records, in the twenty-seventh century B.C., one of their emperors had used the south-pointing chariot device to steer an army out of a fog.

From the western viewpoint the Chinese did two things backward.

1. They steered an army instead of a ship.
2. Their compass pointed south. The needle of the compass was a magnetic fish with a big tail. They thought that the head was pointing south, not realizing the tail was pointing north. With this device their journey to America would have been greatly expedited.

Fixed rudder

Joseph Needham of England in his five-volumes of *Science and Civilization in China* has opened up researches in Chinese history which may eventually change all our ideas of Chinese accomplishments in past ages.

Prof. Needham has gone a long distance toward proving that the Chinese were probably the fathers of inventions which we have hitherto credited to ourselves. For example, the Greeks and Romans did not develop the fixed rudder. The Chinese had it at an early time … and they also fenestrated[1] it for easier usage when many Westerners had more primitive transportation.[2]

The crossbow

Needham tells us that the crossbow was much more ancient and widespread in China than in Europe. In China it formed the standard weapon of Han armies, and was in continuous use from the fourth century before Christ onwards. This is Needham's opinion but we feel that the Chinese had the crossbow even long before.

Shen Kua, who lived in the eleventh century A.D., tells a remarkable story:

> When I once dug in the garden of a house at Haichow I unearthed a crossbow trigger-mechanism (a crossbow-like instrument). On looking at the whole breadth of a mountain, the distance on the instrument was long; on looking at a small part of the mountain-side, the distance on the instrument was short (because the cross-piece had to be pushed further away from the eye, and the graduation started from the further end). The stock of the crossbow was like a rule with graduation in inches and tenths of an inch. The idea was that by (placing) an arrow (across it at different points) and looking past the two ends of the arrow one could measure the degree of the mountain on the instrument, and in this way calculate its height. This is the same as the method of similar right-angled triangles of the mathematicians.
>
> The Thai Chia chapter (of the *Shu Ching*) speaks of a man with his bow drawn and his finger on the trigger "aiming at the target embraced in the graduations" something like the graduation on the crossbow-instrument just described.[3]
>
> In Han times [202 B.C. - 9 A.D.] Prince of Chen, Wang Chung, was very skillful with the crossbow. He could hit the bulls-eye with a 100 percent score ... I once arranged such a "three lengthwise and three crosswise" (grid) on a crossbow ... the result was that my shots were successful seven or eight times out of ten. If graduations are added on the trigger mechanism (itself), the accuracy will be still further improved.[4]

Shen Kua had found an instrument known in Europe as the cross-staff, crossbow or arbalest which had been used for the measurement of heights, breadths and distances. Shen Kua believed that sighting techniques of the Prince of Chen had also involved an instrument with a stock graduated for use as a cross-staff.

It could have been such an instrument that Prince Y used to calculate the actions of the suns. He sailed across the Pacific Ocean with the frailty of a man and daring of a god. At the Grand Canyon, Prince Y had shot the true sun, and taken its measurements. In an astronomical sense, Prince Y did shoot the nine extra suns.

Ancient astrological instruments

In the second chapter of the *Shu King* it is said that Emperor Shun examined an instrument called Suan Ki Yu Heng[5] (2260 B.C.). It was jade used to regulate the governors (i.e., sun, moon, and five planets). It is understood by Chinese and foreign commentators that Shun employed an astronomical instrument. Chinese books on astronomy often showed a complex apparatus of spheroid shape used for astronomical purposes. Until we know ourselves how to make those devices (which I have seen), we reckon it best to accept Chinese statements that they knew how to calculate astronomical matters in ancient times.

For example, the jade astronomical Suan-ki is a most remarkable and complex instrument. It is all on one disc and the outer edge of the ring is very curiously shaped and divided into three sections of equal length, marked off by a deep incision, forming a pointed angle on the inner and a pointed projection at the outer side. Each of these three divisions is indented in such a way that six small teeth of irregular shape project over the edge leaving five slightly curved notches in the interstices. We confess that we do not understand how this instrument was used. Our ignorance does not prevent its being a valid astronomical device. It seems to have been employed in unison with the Tsung, the Pi, the Kuei, and astral crossbow as very effective means of bringing the seasons and directions once again under the control of man's golden hands.

We have studied thousands of jade pieces, and are convinced that the Pi, the Tsung and the Sceptre (which invariably has a constellation, including the pole star on it) were used, in combinations, to arrive at very complicated conclusions concerning latitude and longitude, and other important determinations. An American geographer, Dr. Charles P. Hapgood, was the first person in the West to realize that ancient Chinese knew latitude and longitude.

The quipu

When the Spaniards came to Peru they found no written language in use. They did find the quipu, whose knotted cords were used as records. The following inventions are mentioned in the Chinese *Book of Changes [I Jing]*: nets, ploughshares, markets, boats, carts, gates, pestle and mortar, bow and arrow, houses, coffins, quipu.[6]

This last invention took place, evidently, at least two thousand years before Christ. There is no need or reason to dispute the claim. Its use in

Peru is simply evidence that the Chinese were there at a very early time. The quipu is still in use in Asia. This ancient method of recording has persisted in the Liu-Chu Islands until now.[7]

In the eighth chapter of the *Tao Te Ching* we are told by sages of China who wanted men to go back to the ancient ways that it would be a wonderful thing if: "The people should go back (from writing) to knotted cords, be contented with their food, pleased with their clothes, satisfied with their homes, and happy in their work."[8]

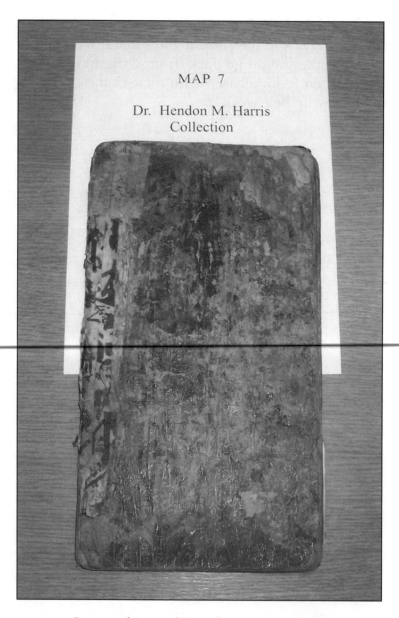

Cover of one of the Harris Map Books

CHAPTER 11

Others Were Involved In Fu Sang

In giving so much credit to the Chinese, we do not wish at all to disparage the contributions of many other nations to the new world. According to Vining, "The Hans were among the oldest of the Chinese races; they occupied the northern part of the empire, overspread Corea (sic), and ultimately became masters of Japan. In the third century of our era, these Han rulers of Japan took possession of Corea (sic), which after the fall of the Han Dynasty in China, appears to have become the general rendezvous of the Han races."[1] Here is a remarkable use of the word "Han" which seems to clearly justify our use of it to include the Chinese, Japanese, and Koreans.

The Chinese accounts agree that the normal passage to America would go by way of Korea, then from Japan to the country of Dah Han, and from there would go southeast towards California. The groups arriving in Fu Sang would include not only Chinese but also Koreans and Japanese. I think it would have been impossible to exclude peoples as vigorous and ambitious as the Japanese and the Koreans from participating in the life of Fu Sang in the early periods especially in that both had access to the Japan (Kamchatka) current.

Japanese brought their pottery to South America at an early time. The existence of Japanese-type armor all the way around from Honshu, past the Aleutians, the northeast coast down to the Columbia River, and down to Mexico[2] proves to my mind that Japanese were always present in Fu Sang to some degree. Cyrus H. Gordon brings to our attention the theory that the Japanese came to Ecuador as early as 3000 B. C. and brought their Jomon pottery. Dr. Manly P. Hall, philosopher and scholar of world culture, told us that the Japanese government presented to the Peruvian government a bronze statue of the First Emperor of Japan—in honor of those Japanese navigators who long ago sailed across the Pacific and colonized ancient Peru. It is the understanding of Japanese that the Incas of Peru were descended from Japanese explorers. Dr. Hall informed us that the same Falcon symbol used in the Imperial Incan coat of arms was present in the high Japanese insignia. There are also many similarities between Japanese and Mayans.

The kings of Fu Sang also had customs and names that were found in early Korea. Hui Shun acknowledged that the top three ranks in the Fu Sang Kingdom, probably in Peru, had names that were identical to those used in Korea. Why would the top nobility in Peru (or perhaps Mexico) be called 'Dah Tui-lu' if the Koreans hadn't been there to give them those names which were identical to the names used in Korea?

As to those from India, I have no quarrel with Ebin's stories of their early voyages to America, before or about the time of Christ's birth. Realizing the sophistication of their shipping, this is more than probable. Of the Annamese and Indonesian ventures one feels a certain shakiness. Many things attributed to them could have been accomplished by the East Indians. We feel certain that the East Indians were in Fu Sang after 458 A.D. as we will point out later.

Furthermore we see no reason to doubt the Jewish journeys to Bat Cave in Tennessee after the failure of the last desperate Hebrew oppositions to the Romans. And the expeditions of the Phoenicians, Romans, and Carthaginians could have taken place, although we strongly suspect their arrival by no means guaranteed they would return, or even survive.

Coming closer to modern times, the arrival of Madoc, Irishmen, Scots, Norsemen, and even the late-comer Columbus should not be either too greatly doubted or lauded. I have always looked with amusement on those who desperately tried to keep everybody out so the American Indians could have a chance at a do-it-yourself civilization.

I do not think the guests were longed for, but there was little that could be done by the American Indians to prevent their arrival. It is highly possible that the Aztec custom of eating comely captives was encouraged by the rather frequent arrival of greedy fat foreigners who found themselves regretfully denied exit permits after they had once seen the plunderable wonders of Fu Sang. Stout Cortez, himself, would have made a pleasant meal for Montezuma had not the menu been clouded by the Aztec's fears that the Spaniard was the Second Coming of Quetzalcoatl! All of which gives food for sober reflection.

We do not seek to deny anyone participation in the civilization of old "America." However, it should be obvious that it was on the western seaboard of "America," where Asiatic waves came in, that we see the most significant evidences of true heights of civilization.

No, everyone who played a part in the game of early Fu Sang should be given credit. But no more then is due them. It is the matter of primacy and proportion that causes us now to stand up. It should be obvious to all that there is one nation which plays an overriding part in the whole history of Fu Sang.

The Chinese Records of the *Shan Hai Jing, Shu Ching,* and indisputable proofs of the corroborating ancient maps show that it was the Chinese who always acted out in those early times … the main part in the drama. They were the planners. They fathered tribe after tribe. They kept the contacts and made the surveys, the maps, and the military campaigns.

The Chinese fatherhood, customs, traditions and contacts were written first and forever into the history, colonies, high deeds, and bodies of the American Indians. The influence of others was later, casual, incomplete, or uncertain.

Our attitude towards American Indians and East Asians

The same unfair, cruel attitude that our forefathers revealed to the American Indian has also, more than most of us realize, been shown in times past to the people of Asia. We are thoroughly indignant about the whole thing and wish to publicly wash our hands of any complicity in it.

While I do not at all believe that Indians should be given payment several times in succession for the same land, it should seem obvious that all their rights must be strictly and generously maintained. It seems unthinkable that we still allow greedy storekeepers to rob the original inhabitants of the land—that we permit American Indians to live in rank poverty while we subsidize our former enemies with lavish overseas grants. The Indian was not a perfect person, but there can be no question that our fathers often broke solemn treaties that the simple, honest [Native Americans] had accepted at face value.

We must have rightly seemed like devils to people whose women and children could be raped and slaughtered at the slightest provocation, their land repeatedly stolen without excuse and against covenants. Our people who poured westward cared little for the Indians and thought the "only good Indian was a dead Indian." We do not believe that any minority in America should make itself a nuisance to the majority, but if ever there was a minority group in our country that rightly deserves special treatment, it seems to us that the American Indians have a prior claim that cannot be denied by conscientious citizens.

This same attitude, this unwarranted unreasonable attitude of superiority toward other people, appeared in our Asian policies until only a few decades ago. It was commonly thought by foreigners that the Chinese were incapable of many things in which they had clearly excelled us in times past. As an instance of the incredible arrogance, I have a map in which the reader is told that certain areas on the map were totally unknown to Chinese at all times. Imagine how indignant you would feel if you were solemnly told that all your ancestors were morons and incapable of travel! The very areas marked on the maps as "unknown to Chinese at all times" were for thousands of years traversed only by people of Asian stock. But now the day has come when we must look with respect to the great vibrant nations of Asia.

Dr. Harris viewing antique Chinese coins in the marketplace.

CHAPTER 12
Further Proofs of Early Asian Relationships in Fu Sang

Ancestor worship in Central America

Cyrus H. Gordon gave the following information concerning the cultic-mushroom stones that are common in Middle America. These stones are almost certainly evidence of Chinese ancestor worship practiced on this continent. Gordon mentions Dr. Dennis W. Lou, Professor of History at the State University of New York, who has compared the America mushroom stones with the ancestor stones of his native China:

> The form was apparently suggested by resemblance of the mushroom to a male [reproductive organ], representing the male ancestor. Dr. Lou rightly maintains that ancestor worship makes more sense than mushroom worship, and his view is substantiated by a series of mushroom stones in the Archaeological and Ethnological Museums in Guatemala City. One of these stones has a man's face on the stem, confirming Lou's theory that the stones stand for people. Another Guatemala Museum stone has a whole human head instead of the mushroom stem, so the button of the mushroom looks like a turban.
>
> That ancestor worship fits into the Maya scheme is confirmed by living Maya usage. In Chichicastenango, Guatemala, Maya and other Indians pray to their ancestors in the church under the aegis not of Catholic priests but of their own witch doctors. On little platforms set up in the aisles of the church they light single candles for female ancestors and double for male ancestors. Rose petals are spread and liquor sprinkled to propitiate the ancestral spirits.
>
> It is interesting that it took a Chinese scholar familiar with the phenomenon of ancestor worship to connect this link of Middle America to the Far East.[1]

Chinese writing in Mexico

In speaking with Dr. Manly P. Hall, philosopher and scholar of world culture, we were overjoyed to learn that Chinese tablets inscribed with words from China have been dug up from fifty feet underground by archaeologists at Mexico City. This reinforces the contention that Chinese have long had a continuing relationship with Mexican peoples.

A find of ancient Chinese coins in British Columbia

An 1882 Canadian newspaper reported:

> What if antiquarians are able to prove that the Chinese were the earliest settlers of this continent? That from the loins of the children of the "Flowery Kingdom" are descended the native tribes whom the white pioneers found possessing the land? This theory has been often advanced. A few weeks ago a party of miners, who were running adrift in the bank on one of the creeks in the mining district of Cassiar made a remarkable find. At a depth of several feet the shovel of one of the party raised about thirty of the brass coins which [were the type used for] currency in China for many centuries. They were strung on what appeared to be an iron wire. This wire went to dust a few minutes after being exposed but the coins appeared as bright and new as when they left the Celestial mint. They have been brought to Victoria, and submitted to the inspection of intelligent Chinamen, who unite in pronouncing them to be upward of three thousand years old. They bear a date about twelve hundred years anterior to the birth of Christ. And now the question arises as to how the coins got to the place where they were found. The miners say there was no evidence of ground having been disturbed by man before their picks and shovels penetrated it; and the fact that the coins are little worn goes to show that they were not long in circulation before being hidden or lost at Cassiar. Whether they were the property of Chinese mariners who were wrecked on the north coast about three thousand years ago, and remained to people the continent; or whether the Chinese miners who went to Cassiar seven or eight years ago and deposited the collection where it was found for the purpose of establishing for their nation a prior claim to the land may never be known. But the native tribes of this coast resemble the Mongolian race so closely, that one would not be surprised at any time to hear of the discovery of yet more startling evidences of the presence of Chinese on this coast before the coming of the whites.[2]

Horses in ancient Alaska

The *New Records of the Tang Dynasty* says: "Ta Han borders on the north of Kuh; it is rich in sheep and horses. The men are tall and large[3] and this has given the name Ta Han (i.e. Great Giants) to their country. This kingdom and Kuh both [share a common boundary] with Kieh-Kiah-sz', and therefore they were never seen as guests (in our court). But during the reigns of Ching-Kwan and Yung-hwui (A.D. 627 - 656) they presented sable skins and horses, and were received. It may be that they have come once since that time."[4] This is ancient Alaska.

The existence of horses in Alaska knocks all theories of a non-horse North America into a cocked hat. The *Shan Hai Jing* also talks about certain things that were "good for horses" in Fu Sang. Probably the earliest explorers brought their own wiry ponies for aids in the vast explorations.

Ancient Chinese military expeditions in America

Kih Kiun's *Bamboo Book* tells us in its comments on the *Shan Hai Jing* that P'oh Shu Tsz went on a military expedition in the Eastern Sea for a full three years. Since the discussion is about places in Fu Sang, we can plausibly entertain the accuracy of the statements.[5] The campaign probably took place millennia ago.

Prof. James Wei, of Hong Kong, tells us that Emperor Li Pien of Southern Tang Dynasty sent General Hu Tsung Tan to a tribe 10,000 sea miles east of Korea, a tribe called Four Fairy Peaks.[6] This was possibly Temistitan on the Mexican heights. The year was 939 A.D. and approximately coincided with the Toltec taking of Tula, thereafter Chichen Itza.

The *China News* tells us concerning this matter: "The Taoists monks of the Sung Dynasty used to boast of breaking the country of Fu Sang with one blow of the fist. It could have meant the breakthrough to America."[7]

The Immigration to China from Fu Sang?

Vining says,

> I have sometimes thought that a great mystery might be concealed in the origin of the old Chinese with black hair, who arrived from the north (it is not known from what country) at the banks of the Yellow River—not as primitive men, but as the representatives of a ripened civilization—who avoided any intermixture with the

native population, and who always turned themselves toward their fatherland to seek for light. If it should be unquestionably proved that Fu Sang is indeed America, and if the first ideas which the Chinese had of that region should appear lost in the most remote antiquity, would not a strange enigma be presented to us for solution?[8]

Russian studies of the Asian American problem

On July 11, 1970, a United Press International dispatch from Moscow printed in the *New York Times,* Sunday July 12, 1970, a Soviet scientific report which suggested that it was really the Asians who discovered America.

The new challenge to Columbus rests partly on ancient Tibetan maps, and partly on the use of tobacco among Asians. In reporting the findings of Lev Gumilev and Bronislav Kuznetsov who were described as Leningrad specialists in oriental antiquity, Tass, the Soviet Press Agency said that the honor of discovery of the Americas possibly belonged to ancient Asian adventurers.

The Agency said that the specialists interpreted references in ancient Tibetan maps to a land lying far across the Eastern Sea, meaning America. This, Tass added, is substantiated by the fact that the purely American word, tobacco, penetrated a number of oriental languages and dialects in antiquity.[9]

Customs that tie China and Fu Sang together

Mencius tells us that in 2250-05 B.C. a king did not ascend the throne until after a three-year period of seclusion. On the death of Yao, Shun retired into seclusion for three years before ascending to the throne. On Shun's death, Yu, who had been minister of Public Works and served under Shun seventeen years, likewise went into retirement for three years before seating himself on the royal throne.

In Kuen 327, Hui Shan told that the king of Fu Sang did not assume the responsibilities of State until three years after the death of the preceding ruler. If this does not tie Fu Sang together with the custom of ancient China I know not where we can find greater corroboration.[10]

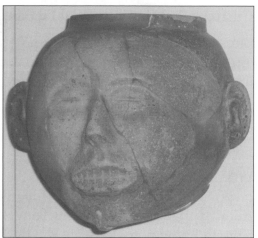

Asian features on faces of artifacts on display at
the Smithsonian's National Museum of the American Indian.
Photos taken in 2006 by Dave Rees.

CHAPTER 13
The Indians

Hopi and Chinese resemblances

I think it important to point out that Hopi women once wore their hair, and wear it to this day for ceremonies, as the Chinese wore it in the Tang period—around 700 A.D. or earlier. The Hopi have a tradition that they were told by their ancestors not to change their hairstyle, because future generations would be able to identify them by their hair.

The traditional male way of wearing hair was to have hair long in the back, and tied in a knot in a fashion similar to that of pre-Tang China. Hopi called the knot a "Chongo." We ask, is it not a strange similarity that "Chong toe fah" means long hair in Chinese?

Mogollons and Others

Mogollons included both the Black People and the White People. We believe both the Hopi and Mogollons were by ancestry Chinese.

> Of all the American tribes, the most civilized are situated near the coast which faces China. In the region of New Mexico there are found tribes that have houses of several stories, with halls, chambers, chamber and bath-rooms. They are clothed in robes of cotton and of skin: but that which is most unusual among savages is that they have leather shoes and boots.[1]

Now this, of course, is a reference to the Pueblos who were central Asian in origin, and it is correct that the greatest work of the Chinese was in the Pueblo lands and the south regions rather than in California. But the Chinese by no means neglected this state.

In Southeastern California there was a community of Indians known as the Owens Valley People. While the area was not suited for a large population there was at least enough land and water to make life livable for a community. In the 1920s the anthropologist Julian H. Seward studied the Owens Valley Piute. Near this area important petroglyphs [writings on rocks] have been found in tremendous numbers.

Seward found there were permanent clusters along the pinon zone. In this area there were highly advanced methods of irrigation which other Indians knew nothing of yet were practiced here in a sophisticated fashion. Olivia Vlahos says, "Nobody knows how or when the Owens Valley people learned about irrigation. Nobody knows whether it was introduced from the outside or invented from within. To the west, in coastal California, Indians in the old days were acorn gatherers, hunters and fishermen."[2]

It should be quite evident that, even as the elaborate irrigation procedures of Asia were taught further south, an occasional drop of wisdom from across the Pacific fell on the Indians of California.

Snake Indians

In an old fragment regarding the *Walam Olum*, the following is said:

> The name Snakes has been applied to several historic western North American Indian groups; numerous Shoshonean bands of eastern Oregon, northern Idaho, and Wyoming are referred to in the early days as Snake Indians. More pertinent for us, however, is the fact that various Algonquian-speaking groups designate inimical Iroquoian and Siouan-speaking tribes as "adders" or "real serpents," hence "snake seems to be an Algonquian metaphor for any people regarded as enemies, rather than for a particular linguistic group or tribe.[3]

Let us notice that the writer confirms the fact that there have been several tribes called Snakes among the western Indians. It is on the coast where the Chinese landed that we find them. He names several of these tribes, beginning with the Shoshones of Oregon. We believe that the name Shoshone comes from shuh shuh which means "snake, snake" in Chinese.

But why were the tribes of Chinese origin given this peculiar title? The answer, we believe, is that the Chinese were the dragon people and thought of themselves as descendants of the Celestial dragon. There are no dragons in America. Yet, there are multitudes of snakes. So it is an easy substitute.

The Snake tribes are the very ones that have Chinese blood, according to the tests, and is confirmation of what we are saying. The Snakes were Asiatic, and the blood tests prove it. We know that the Sioux Indians were Asiatic. Once again, I believe that Sioux is just another derivation of "shuh" which we mentioned before.

Algonquins called their foes Snakes in the same way that an enemy will use a name or nickname against them. If their name is Stone he will say: "You have a stone heart, don't you?" In other words, they used their REAL NAME to slur them.

The Country of Refined Gentlemen

According to the Harris Fu Sang map, the country of the Refined Gentlemen is California. They were north (and probably west) of She-pi's Body, which I believe was the ancient Indian tribal symbol. The next area was Kan-yu's Body which was a representation of another early Indian group.

They were well-dressed people with excellent clothing—fine caps, beautiful sashes, and swords. Their wives and children were decked out in exotic garments and there was no lack of food in their houses. For pets they had Mexican tigers. When they sat at their meals these beasts reclined on each side of them.

The Refined Gentlemen, says the *Shan Hai Jing*, were very gentle and did not quarrel. They loved flowers, and their gardens were full of blooming plants.

Ms. Mertz tells us:

> On the California coast, due north of Los Angeles, and at approximately the spot where Point Hueneme stands, where in my opinion Hui Shan landed, California records disclose an ancient Indian site. For what little we know today, the place bears evidence of being a holy one, a place of sacrifice.

> Moving inland from Point Hueneme, we find sites, legends and traditions from the coast to the Rockies, with civilizations that date far back of the Spanish Conquest to an ancient and highly cultured past. The Cochise, a nomadic Indian people, roamed over considerable portions of what is now Southern California, Arizona, New Mexico, Sonora and Chihuahua. The Cochise are thought to have been there as early as 3000 B.C.[4]

The Cochise, with their ancient civilization and courteous ways may well have been the people of the Land of the Refined Gentlemen. The Arabs of the Arabian desert exemplify punctilious of matters of courtesy, despite their nomadic life. There is no reason this could not have been true in earliest America.

Furthermore, the polished manners of those ancient aristocrats ... the Refined Gentlemen ... and the respect in which they were regarded by the writer of the *Shan Hai Jing* makes it more than likely that they too were Chinese.

Kuh Chi in Chinese means "polite." Gwoah or kuo is Chinese for nation. I believe that their original name was probably Kuh chi kuo "the polite nation" and thus this became "Cochise" in the process of times.

The story of the emperor of China deliberately appropriating the title "Land of Gentlemen" and giving the title to the Koreans is told in the Notes of Chau Ju-Kua's book by Friedrich Hirth and W. W. Rockhill.

> It was in A.D. 737 that Hing Shou was sent on a mission of condolence to Korea on the death of Hing-Kuang, king of Sin-Lo. When the deceased king's son Chong King ascended the throne, the envoy was instructed to state in the name of the Emperor that Sin Lo was styled the Country of the Gentlemen, because its people understood poetry and literature....[5]

As early as B. C. 122 Liu An had referred to a Country of Gentlemen in the East but of course he was looking across the ocean with the writers of the *Shan Hai Jing*. With the Chinese terming Korea BOTH the "Land of the Manifestation of the Dawn" and the "Land of Gentlemen,"... it is no wonder that this threw everyone off the track. Then when Japan took both the name Fu Sang and the title "Land of the Rising Sun" the whole matter became obscured for hundreds of years.

Toltecs and Aztecs

America's Ancient Civilizations stated:

> It took centuries for the European artisans and engineers to erect cathedrals, despite the fact that they possessed highly efficient steel implements and facilities which the Aztecs lacked, yet no European cathedral can begin to compare with the vast pyramids

and temples of the Aztecs, either in the quantities of stone used in their construction or richness of stone sculptures and carvings.

The Aztecs had not only constructed dozens of these but had been offering sacrifices on their altars for more than 100 years before Cortez arrived on the scene. In addition they had conquered numerous races and built a huge capitol city, had constructed splendid causeways across Lake Tezcoco, had perfected cylindrical and numerical systems, and had developed a highly advanced civilization, all in the space of 200 years or less.

This Taiwanese man has features one might expect on a native American.

The only plausible or logical explanation of the Aztecs' seemingly impossible rapid advancement is that they had brought their civilization with them, that they already possessed their fully developed and highly complicated religion, their amazing astronomical knowledge, their numerical and cylindrical systems, their arts, crafts and practically everything else all inherited from the Toltecs whom they claimed were their ancestors. In fact the first Aztec ruler was a Toltec.[6]

Proof through blood and physical features

William C. Boyd, in his outstanding work[7] in 1950 found that eight native American tribes have Asiatic type blood. The Kwakiutl Indians of British Columbia, the Pueblo Indians of New Mexico, Hopi, Navajo, Sioux of South Dakota, Shoshone, and the Maya of Yucatan, and the Mapuchis of Chile. Many other Indian groups probably have Asiatic blood, but these above-mentioned tribes are demonstrably and clearly Asiatic in origin.

The Maya had the epicanthic eye-fold, and the Mongolian blue spot near the base of the spine, which is almost certainly Chinese.

Maya men wore their hair long with a bare spot burned on the top of the head. Their hair was braided and wound around the head except for a queue which fell behind. I remember as a child seeing the burned places on Chinese heads and similar hairstyles.

Chinese traces in the Indian languages

Chinese of 4000 years ago was probably a much simpler language than the one that now exists. Of course, over thousands of years we would expect the languages to drift far apart. Each language was subject to foreign elements, mutations and additions indigenous to its own area and experience. This has been true of the Indo-European languages. How much more, two languages from the same tree separated by 6000 miles of Pacific and millenniums of time. Yet we would rightly expect to find some evidences that prove the original contact, and they are definitely there.

In much of the speech of the American Indians we find lingual ties and relationships that prove the presence of the Chinese. The customs, speech, and actions of the Indians are replete with Chinese habits, superstitions and mores. One famous Mexican said to an American visitor, "You are looking at a Chinese." To a great extent Diego Rivera was right.

I have been struck, as I studied Maya time-names, by the strong resemblance to Chinese names. The Chinese called a day a Tin and the Mayans called it a Kin. The Chinese had a Yueh for a month and the Maya a Uinal. The Chinese had Nien for a year and the Mayans a Tun.

At least five of the twenty Maya day names are Chinese in form. The first Maya day is Ik and the Chinese name I. We also find the names Kan-Chuen-Ben-and Men all of which I believe are Chinese, and the month name Chen is probably also Chinese.

Furthermore, having been raised on the plains of Henan in China, I had the uncanny feeling that I was dealing with Maya Chinese people whose ancestors had come from "MY" district in China! I think I was correct in this supposition, for it is well known that my area of Kaifeng is the most ancient part of the Han Empire. The very region where the Chinese first formed their civilization and took up united action against the rampaging waters—this general area from which Yu and Y and Huan Tow had journeyed to do their great exploits in America.

An ancient Peruvian drank his chicha before going to work and a Chinese would chih cha (drink tea) before going to his tasks.
Chinese called servants puren and the Incas called the lower classes puri.

Each Inca couple got a topu of land at marriage and the Chinese couple got a tipi. Probably the Indian "teepee" came from the Chinese "tipi."

The South American term kue hua means "countrymen of Chinese Ancestry" in the Chinese language spoken by the Central Chinese of ancient times.

The word llama sounds like lao ma which means "old horse" in Chinese and would fully justify Hui Shan's account of horses in Fu Sang.

H. Prescott says "Othomi language, which covers a wider territory than any other but the Mexican, shows a very singular affinity to the Chinese."[8]

The Incas called a baby a wa wa which is the same name given to infants in China to this day.

The invaders of Northern Yucatan in the so called post classic time were Nahuatl speaking people according to Morley. (Ancient Maya p. 20) In Chinese Dah Hua means "great Chinese."

In Yucatan the West was called Chi-Kan. The Chinese call the West Shi-Fong.

The Fu Sang medicine man was called Ah men and the Asiatic Sha Mun was also a healer.

The Chinese said that the shun or god Pan Koo created the world. According to the Mayan belief Hunab Ku created the earth.

The Mayans believed that there were nine gods of the lower world called Bolontiku. In Chinese the Jo shun dee you means the Nine Gods of Hell.

The Mayan Lord of Death was named Ah Puch. Dah Suh in Chinese means Great Death.

Native lore

Vining tells us:

> There exists in Mexico a tradition of Hui Shan's visit. This gives
> his name and title of Hui Shan, Bhikshu, as Wi-Shi-Pecocha; tells
> the district of the Pacific coast upon which he landed; describes
> his complexion, his beard, and his dress; related the doctrines that
> he preached: mentions the success that he met in his mission, and
> states the reason for his return to Asia. Traditions also exist of the
> visit of the party of Buddhist priests mentioned by Hui Shan, from
> whom he seems in some way to have become separated.[9]

CHAPTER 14

Head Alterations in the Old World and the New

Decorated Heads

The Maya Corn God is represented as a young man with a tall head and a beautiful hairdo. In the Sanskrit we find Manjusri, a bodhisattva whose name is taken from Manju (beautiful) and Sri (good fortune, virtue, majesty, Lord—epithets applied to a god). His later Chinese name was Man Soo Shih Li.

From his East Indian name, the Chinese derived several other names for him. The first signified "wonderful (or beautiful) head." Also, he is known as Pu So, universal head, and as Roo So, which is glossy head. Further, he is Jing So, revered head.[1]

He is represented as a youth—eternal youth. His present abode is given in Chinese lore as east of the universe,[2] in a place known as Ching Liang San, the clear and cool mountain (which suggests the mountains of Central Mexico). This location is also called Bowdzoo, "precious abode," or "abode of treasures." Any one who knew of Cortez' journey into the Aztec Capital realized that early Mexico was rich with gold and other precious things.

Manjusri is mentioned in China as early as the fourth century, and in the *Lotus Sutra* he frequently appears, especially as converter of the daughter of the Dragon-king of the Ocean.[3] It is very interesting to this writer that his traditional abode is in the northeast. It was towards the northeast that the earliest explorers journeyed on their way to Fu Sang.

On the Harris map the Maya area is designated as Huan Tow Gwoah or land of the beautifully decorated heads. We know Maya leaders had long heads, artificially lengthened and charmingly coiffured. This custom was perhaps confined to the leadership class but was a distinctive Maya characteristic.

Elongated skull from Mexico.

Werner informs us that ancestors of the Chinese who settled in northwest China about the twenty-third century B.C. or before appear to have practiced the custom of flattening heads of their infants. The desired shape was a pyramid, broad and large in the lower part, tapering toward the top—opposite of the dome shaped head and pointed lower face often associated in the West with an intellectual brain.[4]

The ideal shape of the ancient Chinese head is pictured in many portraits of their early emperors and heroes. The virile and real emperors described in the *Bamboo Book* had a remarkable type of head. Hwang-Ti's forehead "tapered like that of a dragon." Chuan Hsu possessed a head as broad "as a shield and pointed like a spear." Emperor Yao's face was "sharp above and broad below." Yu the Great had a large mouth and a tiger's nose, and a pointed head. Ch'eng T'ang's face was "broad and tapered upwards."[5]

The records of Han Dynasty state that a Korean tribe, the Ch'en Han, flattened the heads of their newly born children with stones. The Buddhist Pilgrim Hsuan Tsang of the T'ang Dynasty (A.D. 602-664) put it on record that the custom existed in Kashgar.[6]

The Sulu Islanders, whose Sultan dispatched an embassy to China in A.D. 636 followed the same custom.[7] Both Manchurians and Koreans flattened heads. We find the tapered head conspicuous in pictures of emperors and empresses during the Yuan Dynasty as depicted in the *Li tai ti wang Hsuang*. The manchus were still tapering their heads at the beginning of the twentieth century.

My friend Stephen Wu of Taipei, one of China's great calligraphers, pointed out to me that the Chinese phrase "decorated head" originally was a head with eyes, nose, mouth, and wavy hair, or hat. There are several other examples of these Chinese characters showing decorated heads. Notice the strong resemblance of the early Chinese decorated heads to the Maya leadership types.

Professor Charles Feng of Taipei tells us that there are two basic meanings for huan, "head." Huan can either imply either a happy, or festive (decorated) head, or a long horse-like head. It may well be that the second of these meanings is the more exact. According to Chinese records[8] Emperor Yao, who lived 2300 years B.C. had a minister named Huan Doe, who was exiled. He jumped into the South Sea and drowned. Then his son Huan Tow was sent by the emperor to the South Sea to worship his father.

This story is particularly remarkable because the country of Huan Tow is the Maya territory, according to the early Korean Harris Fu Sang Map, and a passage to Fu Sang, south of Luzon, could be called a trip to the South or Southeast. The Chinese often spoke of East instead of Northeast, and South instead of Southeast.[9] I am now convinced that the Chinese were not only fathers of the Mayan but maintained contact with them, at least sporadically, over a period of several thousand years. The maps prove this definitely.

There is an ancient map of the Korean series, without date or author, at the Ecole des Langues Orientales Vivantes in Paris, 43x63 cm. which shows the Yucatan peninsula jutting into the Pacific Ocean instead of Gulf of Mexico. This old map has the phrase "land of decorated heads," just under the Yucatan area.[10] This map is very helpful because it clearly shows that Hui Shan regarded Yucatan as the place of decorated heads and that he thought he would have to go east to return to Asia.

In sending Huan Tow to the south, the emperor, according to the ancient maps' layout, would expect him to strike land in the southeast. No doubt the emperor would feel guilty over Huan Doe's sad death, according to Chinese custom. So in sending Huan Tow to worship his father's spirit he would normally show great generosity to the dead man's son, and probably allow him to take one of the best ships available. He would also allow him to take his full family and all the servants and soldiers Huan Tow asked for.[11]

That they spent many years "worshipping Huan Doe's spirit" in Maya land was only natural. Polite excuses sent to the emperor for delay in returning would have been understood. All the more, if they asked for the status as a "colony" of China and sent a bit of tax money. All Maya noblemen had long decorated heads like their ancestor Huan Doe!

Head flattening

We are told that the Chinese character "shih" composed of "stone" and "head" which means great or eminent, is supposed to allude not only to the practice of head flattening itself but to the status of those who observed it, or the esteem in which the custom was held in ancient times.

The reasons assigned for this at first sight senseless custom are various, but the most general one seems that it distinguishes taper-heads from square-heads. The former are therefore regarded superior. In most cases it would be the king and his family who would be imitated, either out of fear, flattery, or fashion, as the case might be.

I think that the wish to imitate the "ruling" shape of head was the cause of the adoption of the custom in China, or in Babylon, or whatever place the ancestors of the Chinese lived in."[12]

At Mexico City it is possible to see examples in the National Museums of the long artificially lengthened heads of Maya nobility. It should be constantly remembered that this "brain-extension" type of cranium was NOT for the common people. Its specific reason was to distinguish nobility from commoners.

The ancient Chinese (and other rulers) in ancient Fu Sang made no pretense of democracy in their relations with ordinary folk. The "difference" of the leaders was a matter to be prized, and increased. If it took a different type of head to show that you were dealing with an aristocrat, then lengthen the head and beautify it with decorations.

Trepanation

In the fourth century A.D. the *Hsin Thang Shu* says, (ch. 221B) "They (the people of Ta-Chin which is Europe) have clever physicians, who by opening the brain and extracting worms, can cure mu-sheng (a sort of blindness)."[13] This is repeated by the *Wen Hsien Thung Khao*. Needham says he believes this is the solitary instance of any attention consciously paid in Chinese writings to early Western medical science.[14]

Chinese physicians seem to have been fascinated by this particular operation. The *San Kuo Chih* of the third century told about a very remarkable offer. The Wei Emperor Tshao had a serious head problem. A brave and talented Chinese surgeon, Hua Tho, offered to perform a trepanation on the emperor's head. While the monarch refused, it appears that this operation was practiced on the common people with considerable proficiency—not long before the Chinese and East Indians started their trepanations in America—so these practices are important.

In Europe, as early as Hippocrates, a definite description of trepanation was given for a certain form of blindness. "When sight is lost without any apparent disease of the eyes, one should make an incision in the parietal region, dissect the soft parts, trepan the bone, and evacuate the liquid which will come out; this is the treatment, and thus these patients are cured."[15] Needham says, "This information about the medicine and surgery of the West may have reached China through Indian channels. A Buddhist sutra of the Kushan period, subsequently translated into Chinese, has the son of Asoka being cured of blindness by a Bactrian at Gandhara. Another tale (*Sutralamkara*, No. 45) makes the prince the son of a Chinese emperor."[16]

It is likely that trepanation took place in Fu Sang before Hui Shan appeared. [17] In any case, this amazing operation seems to have increased in frequency after the Buddhist priests appeared in America.

Victor Von Hagen tells us,

> Above ten thousand of such trepanned skulls have been found in graves throughout Peru, and in many tombs surgical instruments have been found: obsidian arrow heads shaped for trepanning, bronze tumi knives for cutting, scalpels, pincers, needles for sutures—in short, instruments which can be compared favorably with those known to the Romans. With these instruments Drs. Grana and Rocca actually performed trepanations of the skull on a living patient, using Incan operative techniques (except, of course, with a general anesthetic). They used the Inca form of tourniquet (applied about the whole of the round of the head), and proved the efficacy of the ancient operative techniques. The Indians had forms of gauze and cotton swabs, used a tourniquet, perfected local and perhaps general anesthesia. In addition to skull trepanning, many other forms of amputations were performed (archaeological evidence exists on Mochica pottery); in short, pre-Inca and Inca medicine and surgical practice seem to have been just as advanced, perhaps in many respects more so, than when the gifted Ambroise Pare of France was taking medicine out of its medieval doldrums in sixteenth century Europe.[18]

CHAPTER 15

Official Chinese Records of the Fu Sang Reformation (458-498 A.D.)

In the fifth century A.D. a group of East Indian Priests went to Fu Sang with a group of Chinese, Japanese, and Koreans. Subsequently the laws and customs of Fu Sang changed.

The Golden Fifth Century

The fifth century in Europe was the gateway of imminent and inevitable disaster. Christianity had joined with Caesar, to the corruption of both, and was preparing in its debased form to go into that painful era known as the Dark Ages. Slavs, Scythians, and other wild hordes of the North were threatening the entire Roman Empire. Rome itself, old, sick, and dissolute, was tottering to its collapse. Bad government, vice, unrest, and the decay of a Christianity, which had neither the zeal of its forefathers, nor the knowledge of its great-grandsons, caused many to retire into caves and monasteries, to hide themselves from the bitter realities of life. If ever the end of the world seemed close at hand in Europe, it must have seemed so in the fifth century.

If we had turned our eyes to the East we would have found a far different picture.[1] We would have seen a teeming fifth century India, vibrant with purpose and potential. Buddhism was strong and, though persecuted, was advancing. The fifth century in India was a time when many men still strongly believed the basic teaching of the man who had sat under the Bo Tree. Earnest shamans dreamed that they might carry the religion of Gautama to the ends of the earth. So India sent forth her sons. The most religious nation in the world dispatched emissaries north, south, east and west to proclaim the beautiful but essentially passive and negative doctrines of Buddha. They were successful. Ceylon and Southeast Asia, yes, and great China, Korea, and Japan, were reached and touched to the heart by the spiritual appeal of the new Indian faith.

We must realize that the practical Chinese could never find consolation in Confucianism alone. In fact, it is a misnomer to call Confucianism a religion at all. It is basically a conservative ideology, or social code, which argues that men should keep the good ways of the past in order that there be tranquility in the family, in the government and impersonal relationships. Confucius himself fled from the very idea that he was promoting a religion. On an occasion when one of his pupils asked him a question concerning the way to Heaven, Confucius replied with a reprimand: "I have not yet comprehended all the things upon this earth, and why are you troubling me with inquiries concerning Heaven?"

It was in that century that the nobility of early Indian and Chinese Buddhism was most clearly seen. With humility and discernment the Chinese accepted the teachings of Buddha and expanded on them. They refined the faith with their own purity of thinking and demonstrated its virtues in their lives. It was from such an area of study that our five heroes emerged. As exponents of the finest of India's teaching and as presenters of China at her best, they were to make an impression on the world.

What was it that caused such an impact on the New World at this same time? Henriette Mertz tells us:

> Tremendous spurts of activity in the arts and sciences are known to have taken place shortly after the beginning of the Christian era in southern Mexico, Yucatan and Guatemala. Such things as the corbelled roof suddenly appeared in northwestern Yucatan, in 475 A.D., with no apparent explanation and with no gradual process of evolution leading up to it. It arrived full blown. The calendar came onto the scene at approximately the same time. Great cities such as Chichen Itza and Uxmal rose in spectacular glory.
>
> Speculation started buzzing around among archeologists to find the cause. Some impact from an outside source must have exerted a terrific influence.[2]

Hui Shan

We have the almost incredible, but true, account of Hui Shan's journey to the New World with his four religious companions. The substance of the following account is found in the "Liang Shu," or "Record of the Liang Dynasty," contained in the *Nan-Shih* or *History of the South*, written by Li Yen Shau who lived at the commencement of the seventh century. The Nan Shih forms a portion of the *Great Annals of China*, or *Twenty Two Historians*. Our story is "Kuen 327." Ma Twan Lin copied the account in his *Antiquarian Researches* and published his book in 1321 A.D.

The stories are four-fold. The first account tells of the Fu Sang nation or nations, and a list of their customs and peculiarities. It ends with the terse but all-important announcement of the reforms that took place in that continent in order that the nations so conceived and so dedicated might be Buddhist. This was the beginning of a movement which was a gallant, tremendously dedicated, but, finally abortive struggle to win the New World as a peaceful and happy land of Gautama. For a thousand years they fought a spiritual warfare but toward the end they were rapidly weakening, before the forces of darkness that had come to power. Then came Spain.

Hui Shan's account is the record of the beginnings—the glorious, inspirational commencement of the struggle for the hearts of the American Indians. Its movement of religious and social zeal was like a whirlwind in the early days. It was Joan of Arc, with her bright banner of the Cross, when she first went forth to expel the English from France, in the name of God. It was springtime and friendship and true love for God and man for all the large land of Fu Sang to be filled up with more towers and ziggurats and offerings of flowers. It was a day when you named a whole country (Guatemala) after the great Guatama (Buddha) and the people fell on their knees and thanked heaven for the honor. It was a time when you called another adjoining land by the holy name of Maya, the mother of Buddha.

Behind Hui Shan's simple narrative there are towering cliffs and dazzling chasms. He talks of the expedition with almost superhuman modesty, as though five beggar monks had made a brief visit in a foreign land. He does not speak of the dreadful obstacles, the cities springing up like magic in the forests, the hundreds of thousand of volunteers working with fanatical zeal, the tremendous distances that had to be covered, the amazing astronomical studies. He does not tell how the Mayans became the best fed people in the world, how Teohuatican was being rebuilt, or the stunning plans for the future.

When he came to the Tsi court as an old man he must have been walking in a daze. He had been at the pinnacle of religious and civil power in Fu Sang, and thousands would have cheerfully spilled their blood on his behalf. All of this he had resigned in glorious abnegation and obedience to the Lotus heart of his own creed. Now he would return ... a king in the dust ... to make his last report to the Chinese, who long before had sent him on his way.

When he came to the court his disappointment must have been vast. A weak and unsympathetic monarch was on the throne. The court sycophants looked on him, evidently with lightly veiled contempt. Fu Sang? Who had heard of the place? Was it not a mere poetic fancy? Was this old graybeard not looking for a free meal at royal expense? And so the Lord of Mount Alban, Priest-King of Tula, Prince-Priest of Temistitan, Master Magican of Uxmal and Emperor of the Guatemalans was barely received and grudgingly allowed to present his embassy report. One thing he could do. He could save back the precious presents for a more worthy and understanding king. And so he did.

Three years later he appeared before another and much more sympathetic monarch. This was Emperor Wu of the Liang Dynasty. The year was 502 A.D.

The Record tells us that the old man burst into tears. Let him weep. For is he not the Rain God who waters the flowers! May Quetzalcoatl not shed a few drops of sorrowful remembrance? Now he is but a supplicant in a court where his rusty foreign Chinese appears amusing to the sophisticated courtiers.

The emperor was not unkind, nor fully unbelieving. He was affected by what seemed tears of honest respect. He was amazed at the presents that the old man had brought—a concave mirror (of semi-precious stone) over a foot in diameter. You could see the Palaces of the Sun and the twenty-eight divisions in it. It could set the whole royal pavilion on fire if turned to the sun at certain angles!

He also gave 300 pounds of splendid Fu Sang cloth. Six threads of it could hold up one of the Imperial incense burners of gold and bronze. Perhaps there were gorgeous robes for the queen and the concubines and a golden sash for the monarch with needlework. There was cloth of the fire-rats from Cha Hill that none of the courtiers could set afire, not even with torches or braziers. There were lovely maps of the eastern world showing the locations of the towers and the towers to be with all the countries of Fu Sang in their respective places.

The King of South China was impressed. The man had brought an amazing offering. He should be given a chance to tell what he had to say. So the king appointed four lords of the court to write down the records. This was done with all the pomp and secret mirth that the dignity and the possible fraudulence of the affair demanded.

The four lords did their job, after a fashion. But, probably with secret royal approval they held sessions where the disclosures of Hui Shan were repeated with comic interpolations and mimicking exaggerations. The courtiers were highly delighted with the parodies of this story.

So when Hui Shan told of how there was a Land of the Women where they had snakes for husbands, then derision knew no bounds. Little did the lords of the court realize that far away in Fu Sang the ladies of the Land of Women did have Snake-clan husbands.

It was the account of the Land of Women who had snake husbands that discredited Chinese credibility in Hui Shan's account. It was my location of the Land of the Women on the Harris Fu Sang map that enabled me to complete that series of proofs that will cause Hui Shan to be vindicated.

We must remember that the Bible, or history, or a man's report is not true or false because it is believed or not. It is either true or false in itself. It was impossible for me to start with the assumption that the Buddhist monk Hui Shan was a liar. He rewarded me by proving himself the gentleman and true witness that I assumed he had been.

Hui Shan's mirror offered to the emperor of China

Vining said, "There was also among the presents offered to the emperor a sort of semi-transparent precious stone, cut in the form of a mirror, and of the circumference of more than a foot. In observing the sun by reflection by means of the stone the palace which the sun contains appeared very distinctly." This mirror which Yu Kie mentions was of a material completely strange to the Chinese. Yu Kie calls it a sort of precious stone. Nearly all the historians of Mexico mention the fact that later in history the Aztecs made mirrors of obsidian, which were often ornamented with gold. Bancroft says that their mirror of rock crystal, obsidian, and other stones, brightly polished and encased in rich frames were said to reflect the human fact as clearly as the best of European manufacture.

These mirrors have been found as far north as New Mexico and Arizona, and as far south as Yucatan and Nicaragua, and specimens of them are still preserved in the National Museum of the City of Mexico. They were not only concave but also convex and were of extraordinary beauty and usefulness. The Frenchman Brasseur de Bourbourg says that the priests of Central America by use of the mirror caused the holy fire to descend on the victim, who was immediately consumed.[3] This could only have been done by a concave mirror. We can assume that Hui Shan's mirror was far superior to anything the Chinese had ever seen before.

The Dah Han Mystery

One of the most fought over battlefields of the Hui Shan story has been the location of Dah Han. One of the favorite mis-locations has been Kamchatka. This peninsula of Siberia is a very easy place for Dah Han NOT to be because of the following:

- Kamchatka is somewhat west and above the route which would be normally taken. Men on the way to Fu Sang in slow ships would be inclined to take a long and unpleasant detour. The natural and quick way to America from Korea and Japan does not pass too near Kamchatka. But Hui Shan DID visit Dah Han.

- There would be no earthly or divine reason for going there. Kamchatka never, to our knowledge, has been more than a center for near-barbarians (until recent times).

- The argument against Kamchatka becomes stronger when we find the Strait of Anian mentioned by Marco Polo. It is practically certain that Anian is Dah Han and Dah Han is Anian. Kamchaka has no important strait, but Alaska certainly has a strategic strait separating her from Asia. We find that Anian Strait was renamed, or misnamed Bering Strait. So the Strait of Anian is a very strong argument against the Kamchatka error which has misled many.

- The clinching proof is the Harris Fu Sang map. Right where Alaska is we find Giant or Big Men land. I have the strongest suspicion that these men and their wives were no bigger than anyone else, but dressed in their thick and hairy furs they probably gave the impression of bears for strength and size. The bulky Eskimos—in the old days there was nothing but Eskimo under that first airtight layer —passed as giants.

The English-Chinese dictionary under "giant" gives "ju ren," also "Dah Han." "Dah Han," I mused. Why, that's the same sound as the Chinese name for Dah Han—Alaska. I recalled Da Ren—giants of Alaska.

So it seems likely indeed the Chinese name for old Alaska, "Han people's country," is probably a misunderstanding of the original significance of the term. I had previously, knowing reticence of the Chinese in exploiting their own name, wondered why they would give Alaska such a boldly claimant name as Dah Han. It was the GIANTS, not the Chinese ownership, which brought forth the original Dah Han sound.

Elsewhere we have shown that the British Museum's Fu Sang map misinterprets An-Nan or South Males instead of Southern Peace—clearly a case of misunderstood sounds.

CHAPTER 16

Some Problems of the Asian Impact on America

Problem 1. If these matters of the Asian influence in America are true, why are we just now discovering them? The answer, first of all is that for over 200 years earnest investigators have set forward most of the points we have now brought forward as a unit. However, because of a great prejudice against their being true, these facts have not been accepted heretofore by the scientific community or the general public. The present emphasis on truth in history...the present resolve to treat Asians as full equals, should cause falsehoods to disappear and truth to emerge triumphant.

Problem 2. Do you suppose yourself to be better qualified to set these truths forward? The answer is "absolutely not." They should have been accepted earlier from the mouths of better known people. Because we are now living in an age fairer and more informed, we believe the truth will be accepted and must be accepted. Mr. Truman said there were a million people in America as capable of being president as himself. But God made him president and he expected to fulfill the office to the best of his abilities. Hapgood has pointed out that discerning amateurs often produce the most important discoveries and revelations. We do not claim anything beyond the amateur status.

Problem 3. What will this do to previous history? It is not the student's concern to worry about history, but to be concerned that he is studying true history.

Problem 4. Will the scientists accept these findings? This is an amusing question, because every true man must accept every truth. True science is not reactionary but progressive. Therefore, science will surely be delighted in the enlargement of her boundaries.

Problem 5. Will these findings offend people? I cannot imagine any honest person being offended. It is true that the host of presumed European "discoverers" will lose a bit of prominence but certainly none of their well-earned honors. On the other hand, all Asian nations and North and South American nations will have cause for great pride and rejoicing in the heritage of accomplishments and Asian blood which this record has revealed.

Problem 6. Will it not be long and after many years that these facts will be accepted? We believe they will be rapidly accepted by discerning people and that anyone who opposes them will be an eventual companion of those who maintain that the world is flat.

Problem 7. Do you really have enough evidence? The evidence is absolutely overwhelming. We find Chinese history, Chinese linguistics, Chinese court records, Korean records, maps, history and Japanese customs, history, and geography all blending together with Pacific Coast traditions, Indian legends, Utah artifacts, Hopi history, a thousand Mayan correlations, a thousand Peruvian resemblances, buildings, religious symbols, physical resemblances, towers, clothing, food, facts, legends and superstitions all meshing together, all interwoven together to form a final fabric of truth that simply cannot be unraveled.

This book only touches on some major proofs. We shall allow other scholars to enumerate the full panoply of facts which are at their disposal, in demonstrating the Asian accomplishments in Fu Sang.

About the Author
by Charlotte Harris Rees

Dr. Hendon Mason Harris, Jr.
1916 - 1981

In 1972 my father Dr. Hendon Harris, Jr., found, in an antique shop in Korea, map books containing some fragile maps in classical Chinese. The maps correlate with the *Shan Hai Jing*, a Chinese geography written about 2200 B.C. and quoted throughout Chinese history. The ancient world map in the books places Fu Sang in the location of California. Father wrote a 783-page volume, *The Asiatic Fathers of America*, which contains two books—*The Chinese Discovery and Colonization of Ancient America* and *The Asiatic Kingdoms of America*. He interprets in his book some of the strange place names, compares American Indian words with Chinese, and cites further proofs that America was discovered by the Chinese thousands of years ago. He believed that his old maps were faithful copies of the maps that must originally have been with the *Shan Hai Jing*.

Up to that point Father's life work as a missionary had nothing to do with this discovery. At the same time, it had everything to do with why he was able to read and understand this unusual map when he first saw it. In 1954 he had written this poem:

> Let me play God's game along the road,
> That stretches around the Bend,
> From Hokkaido to the Taj Mahal,
> Until my journey's end.
>
> Let me play God's game with the golden men,
> Who trust in our mutual Lord.
> As long as I live let me go and give,
> The message that's in the Word.
>
> Let me play God's game with all I have,
> And turn my pockets out,
> To lay the last dime on the line,
> Without a sigh or doubt.

> Let me play God's game in joy or grief,
> While hopes and planes still fly,
> And when I'm through let me rest
> Beneath the Eastern sky.[1]

This poem published in one of my father's books of poetry pretty well sums up his life. He had a generous heart, a deep faith in God, and a love for the Chinese people.

Father's parents and grandparents before him had been Southern Baptist missionaries. My grandparents, Dr. Hendon and Florence Harris, set sail on their honeymoon in 1910 to serve in interior China. The family settled in Kaifeng in Honan Province.[2] The city was enclosed in a high wall thirteen miles around, with six gates. During the Sung Dynasty (960-1127) this city, only six miles from the Yellow River, was the capital of China.

Living conditions were difficult in that location. At the time the family lived there, the city of 300,000 had neither a water nor sewage system. Water had to be carried in and sewage carried out daily. After they were repeatedly robbed, the missionary family employed servants to guard the house and help with household chores.[3]

Father was born in Kaifeng in April 1916. He was the fourth of eight children born to the missionary couple. Their first son, William, died at thirteen months. The Harris family felt that the arrival of Hendon, Jr. was an answer to their prayers following William's death.

The Harris children learned Chinese as early as they learned English. They had few toys but they always had books.

Several times there were anti-foreign incidents. Father told of a time when the family was fleeing on a train and he was hidden in a Chinese mailbag. Other than travel by train, the missionaries relied on donkeys for transportation. Several years later, some benefactors sent a Model T Ford from America. Even with a car, the roads were so bad that it took most of a day to travel forty miles.

Father was only a year old when the family took its first furlough home to America. By his second trip to America at age ten he could remember neither his grandparents nor America. From China it is just as close to go west as it is to go east to return to America so that time Grandfather decided to take the family back through Europe. To save money they

The Harris Family, 1933
Back row, left to right: Hendon Jr., Eugene, Hendon Sr., Lawrence
Front row: Florence, Florencita, Helen, Miriam, Richard

booked passage on a tramp steamer, which stopped at many interesting ports, took them past India, up through the Suez Canal, through the Mediterranean and on to Europe. They toured several European countries. Father's love of travel was born.

Before they were able to return to China, the Great Depression struck so they had to remain in America. During the Depression the children were split up for a while. Father and a sister stayed with their grandmother in Birmingham, Alabama, while the rest of the family was in Indiana. Father, age fifteen, had a job selling Bibles. People couldn't pay for the Bibles they had ordered. Father became so discouraged that he ran away from his grandmother's home. The family was frantic. Three months later a disheveled young man was sitting on a park bench in Los Angeles when a kind elderly man just happened to speak to him. The man asked the boy where he was born and was shocked to hear the reply, "Kaifeng, China." The man, another missionary from China, knew my grandparents well. He helped reunite Father with his parents.

It turned out that Father had ridden the rails those months and had experienced some harrowing times. However, he had learned to travel and survive on little, which served him well in later years.

After the Depression my grandparents returned to China for several more terms. By then Father was in college so he stayed in America. However, his heart was still in China.

Father started college intending to be a lawyer but he floundered badly his freshman year. That summer he placed his faith in Christ and felt a call to the ministry. Everything changed. He met life with new zeal.

Understanding Father's simple faith in God is pivotal to understanding about him and the maps. Father explained in *The Asiatic Fathers of America* that his faith in God was akin to his faith in the ability of the Chinese people to have made such an early discovery of America. He had seen God at work in the lives of his parents so he had been able to have faith in God. To a lesser degree Father knew the Chinese people well and was confident of their abilities. He had seen their intelligence and ingenuity so was able to believe that even 4000 years before they were capable of making a trip to America.

Father earned his bachelor's degree from Hanover College and his master's in Divinity from Southern Seminary. In 1940, he married Marjorie Weaver, who also felt called to China. She was a preacher's daughter and a registered nurse.

He earned his doctorate in theology from Northern Baptist Seminary and started four churches in the Chicago area. At that time my parents supported themselves and their ministry on Mother's wages as a nurse and by buying houses, fixing them up while they lived in them, and then reselling them for a profit. In 1946, the year I (their third child) was born, I almost died from pulmonary problems. During that cold Chicago winter, my family was living in a house without interior walls and without adequate heat. Fortunately, that house was soon fixed up and sold.

My parents still yearned to go to China as missionaries. However, by then the political situation in China was volatile. About then, my grandparents left China for the last time—just before the communists took over. The other missionaries who stayed in China were rounded up and sent to prison camps. A seminary classmate of Father's died in one of those prison camps. Still, Father had a burning desire to go to the Chinese people.

> In 1950 when he lived at Chicago he used to go daily to the forest preserves to pray for Taiwan, which was unprotected and expected to be invaded by the Communists in six weeks. Feeling that the Chinese needed his help, he went to the Congressmen in Washington and pleaded with them not to abandon the Free Chinese. Then, with only enough money for a one-way ticket [and an invitation from General Chennault[4]], he left his wife and four children to go on a seemingly ridiculous one-man expedition to help the Chinese in Formosa ... Madame Chiang [Kai-Shek] was touched by his arrival... [Harris] was invited to speak to the Chinese Armies. In his meetings ... more than 38,000 Chinese became Christians during that ... spring and summer. [Soon afterwards] the Communists invaded Korea and Truman sent the Fleet to protect Taiwan.[5]

In 1951 my parents sold their home in Illinois and most of their belongings, then drove west to California with their four children. On the way they raised pledges for their missionary support. When the family reached California, Father went ahead to Taiwan to prepare a place for us. Mother worked for a few weeks in San Francisco in order to earn the money for the rest of our tickets on a freighter to the Orient.

Our arrival in the small village in Taiwan could not have been more electrifying to the villagers than if we had green skin, blue hair, and had arrived in a spaceship. At that time, no one in the village had a television nor had ever seen white, blue-eyed, blonde children. We had non-stop attention. I remember jumping around or making faces just to hear the sighs and giggles. A tall concrete wall had to be built around our yard to give us privacy.

When Father wanted to gather a crowd he would give us drums and cymbals. We would march down the street. When enough people gathered, Father would preach in their native tongue. He taught us Chinese songs about God to sing to the curious crowds. As a young child, I myself prayed to accept Christ and was baptized in the river with the other recent converts.

Father brought home monkeys and a flying squirrel as pets for us and let us take rides on the backs of water buffalo. He insisted that we learn to eat strange and exotic foods and respect Chinese culture. We lived through earthquakes and numerous unusual diseases. Our parents taught us to love God. Father told us wonderful bedtime stories, and wrote songs, a

Hendon and Marjorie Harris and family, 1951

novel, books of poems, and a cantata, in addition to doing his missionary work. His creativity and wonderful sense of humor enriched our lives. Two more children were born to my parents while we were in Taiwan.

Father was literate in several languages including Mandarin. From my earliest memories, he always had a study in our home. He spent hours among his numerous books and the stacks of paper of his research and writing.

Our houseguests ranged from Chinese generals to mountain aborigines, who were just a few years from being headhunters. Our amah (nanny) had bound feet. Occasionally our parents took us on trips up into the mountains of Formosa where we crossed over river gorges on swinging suspension footbridges and rode down the mountains at breakneck speed on narrow gauge handcars. The sights, sounds, tastes, smells, and memories of our childhood had to have been experienced to be understood.

In 1953 when the Americans had 14,500 anti-communist prisoners of war in Korea, [Harris] felt that God wanted him to help the Chinese prisoners. He flew to Korea … and stayed in a missionary's house for two weeks, praying for the Chinese prisoners. At the end of that time Colonel Hanson flew him down to Che-ji-do island, where the POWS were very reluctant to go up to Pan Mun Jom to be interviewed by the [Communists]. [Father spoke in Mandarin to groups] of these prisoners thirty-one times—until all the skin peeled off his face [from sunburn]. [He] told them to trust in God and to resist the North Korean overtures. [He] promised that the Americans would convey them to Taiwan. They believed his words. [Many] signified their willingness to trust Christ and he finally saw most of them alive and well on the island of Formosa."[6]

He was commended by the U.S. Ambassador to China, Karl Rankin, and by Vice President Richard Nixon.[7]

In Taiwan my parents started fourteen chapels and churches,[8] had a Bible training school, an orphanage, and a ministry among the mountain people. As well as reaching out to help save men's souls, on more than one occasion through a heroic act Father saved a man's physical life as well.

Later the family moved to Hong Kong, where they ministered with several other missionaries. The seventh child was adopted there. Raising money for the mission work required Father to travel frequently. In 1967 the family permanently relocated to America to live. Father continued to return to the Orient often. He had been around the globe more than ten times.

All those years Father was an independent missionary. He had no regular paycheck. The ministry was supported by contributions from churches and individuals and by Father's ingenuity. To supplement the contributions, he frequently bought antiques in the Orient and sold them when he went to the States. It was in an antique shop in Korea that he discovered the old and fragile map book. His literacy in Chinese and his familiarity with Chinese literature, the *Shan Hai Jing*, Fu Sang, and world geography allowed him to make the correlation and determine that Fu Sang was America.

Father died suddenly of a stroke in January 1981. He had lived his whole life at full throttle. To the end he believed the Scripture that says, "For by grace are ye saved through faith; and that not of yourselves: it is the gift of God: Not of works, lest any man should boast."[9] He had done many good deeds in life because he was thankful for God's forgiveness of his

**The children of Dr. Hendon M. Harris
and their mother, Marjorie, 1989.
Top row: Mejchahl, Charlotte, Marjorie Florence,
Marjorie, Aurora Dawn
Bottom row: John, Lillian, Hendon III**

own sins and because he loved God and the Chinese people. His actions were not to win God's favor. That he already had.

Father left many books and Oriental antiques to his seven children. Among the antiques were the maps. At probate, we all agreed that the maps needed to be taken to a museum or somewhere to be analyzed and protected.

However, one year passed into the next. Each of us was busy with his own life, and after all, this theory of the Chinese discovering America that long ago seemed too outlandish to be true. Occasionally when we were together, we discussed the maps—wondering whether they really held a great secret. None of us had the time to start the quest of authenticating them.

In 2003, I began this process, cheered on by other family members. I was assisted by some leading experts and made some very interesting discoveries about the maps and Father's theories.

As the facts about the maps began to come in they generated some interesting e-mail traffic between us seven siblings. One brother stated, "Father is taking us on one last treasure hunt." Even as an adult the thought of one last adventure with Father was for me both exhilarating and terrifying. But it was too late to look back. The handcar was already on the track and was careening down the mountain. I held on tight and prayed. Yes, I was able to avoid derailment before I reached truth in the valley below.

Among the books written by Dr. Hendon M. Harris, Jr.

- *The Asiatic Fathers of America* (two books in one volume)
  The Chinese Discovery and Colonization of Ancient America
  and *The Asiatic Kingdoms of America,* 1975

- *Famous Unwritten Letters,* Berne, IN.: Light and Hope Publications, 1956

- *I Predict,* Panchiao, Formosa, 1952

- *Laughter and Tears,* Berne, IN.: Light and Hope Publication, 1954

- *Poems for Grown Up Children,* Berne, IN.: Light and Hope Publication

- *The American Idol,* Wabash, IN.: 1961

- *The River of Heaven* (a novel set in Formosa), ca. 1954

WHAT SPECTACLE
CAN BE MORE EDIFYING
OR MORE SEASONABLE.
THAN THAT OF
LIBERTY & LEARNING.
EACH LEANING ON THE OTHER
FOR THEIR MUTUAL
& SUREST SUPPORT?

James Madison

Dave and Charlotte Rees on one of a dozen trips to the
Library of Congress for research on the Harris map collection.
Dave took most of the recent photos in this book.

AN ENGLISH TRANSLATION OF SECTIONS OF
The Shan Hai Jing

The translation of the *Shan Hai Jing* that follows is based on Edward Vining's translation.[1]

[Editor's Note: This chapter has been included for the benefit of those who wish to study this subject deeper. The words included in parentheses ( ) are possible variations in the translation, or were later additions necessary to complete the sense. Those comments included in brackets [ ] are notes by Chinese commentators—some done hundreds of years after the original text. I myself find the text of the *Shan Hai Jing* easier to comprehend when I eliminate the commentary. Most of the obvious fantasy is in those additions. All brackets in this chapter after this sentence *are not* comments by Rees.]

The *Shan Hai Jing* was cut down and condensed considerably from its larger early form. Book Four contains the record of four surveys from Canada south to Mexico that were made about 2250 B.C. Despite enormous difficulties, the Chinese surveying parties under Yu completed their work.

Henriette Mertz did a bold, scholarly, and commendable job in seeking to identify these ranges.[2] She is probably right in some of her placements. We are particularly impressed by her identification of section three of Book Four as a survey from Mount Fairweather in Alaska to the Santa Barbara Channel in California.

However, these surveys are of lesser importance when compared to the invaluable information that is contained in Books Nine and Fourteen of the *Shan Hai Jing*. Coupled with the Harris Fu Sang Maps we now have the key to early "American" history at an extraordinarily aboriginal date.

Please keep these factors in mind as you read this account:

- This was a real series of surveys in America
- Many of these animals can be identified
- Some of the more fabulous kinds of animals have disappeared, or were mistaken as to real appearance, or are superstitions or tribal gods of the inhabitants. Perhaps some are landmark figures[3]

- This is the earliest known description of Fu Sang, i.e. America

In reading these following chapters, we urge our readers to remember that though some of the accounts seem fabulous AT FIRST, they actually contain many scientific truths. There IS a limited amount of fable and superstition, but the distances have proved accurate, the minerals and fauna have been largely identified, and ancient men made the survey in a very commendable scientific manner.

The Herculean task of charting and analyzing a world that was so greatly different from China should arouse our sympathy. Inevitably, some superstitions and folklore crept into the account. However, the record is sane, and the comments by various writers are in the main sensible and even pleasing.

Fourth Book of the *Shan Hai Jing*
The Classic of the Eastern Mountains
Vining's Translation

1. The beginning of the *Classic of the Eastern Mountains* says that Suh-Chu Mountain on its northern side adjoins Kan-Mei Mountain (or Sunless Mountain). Shih River (or "drinkable water") is found here, a stream that flows northeasterly into the sea. In it there are many water animals called Yung-Yung. These look like brindled cattle [they resembled cattle that are striped like tigers]. Their voices sound like the grunting of swine.

2. Three hundred li to the south, Lei Mountain (or the Mountain of Creeping Plants) is to be found. Upon this there are gems and below it there is gold. Hu River is found here, a stream that flows easterly into Shih River. In this there are many Hwoh-Shi. [These are tadpoles; the book entitled the *Rh'-Ya* calls them Hwoh-Tung.]

3. Three hundred li to the south, Keu-Chwang Mountain (Aspen Mountain) is to be found. Upon this there are many gems and much gold, and below it many green jade stones. Wild animals are found there which look like dogs with six legs. These are called Ts'ung-Ts'ung, the name being given them in imitation of their cry. Birds are also found there which look like domestic fowls, but which have hair like a rat. These are called Tsz' rats. When they are seen, the country is subject to great drought. The Chi River is found here, a stream flowing northerly into Hu River. In this there are many lancet-fish. These are of a dark color, spotted (or striped) with blue, and have a bill like a lancet. [These were originally found in the Eastern

Sea, and they are now found in the Kiang-Tung River also.] Those who eat them are not subject to epidemic diseases.

4. Three hundred li to the south Puh-T'san is found. It has no grass or trees, and no water.

5. Three hundred li to the south Fan-T'iao Mountain (or the Foreign Range) is to be found. It has no grass or trees, but has much sand. The Kien River (Diminishing) River is found here, a stream flowing northerly into the sea. In this there are many Kan fish. (The Kan fish is described as a fish three feet long that is found in the Yan-Tsz' River, having a large mouth and yellowish gills, and a greenish back. [One authority names these "the yellow-jawed fish."]

6. Four hundred li to the south, Ku-Mao Mountain (or the Mountain of the Maiden) is found. Upon this there are many lacquer trees, and below it many mulberry trees, and silkworm oaks. Ku-Mao River is found here- a stream flowing northerly into the sea, in which there are many Kan fish.

7. Four hundred li to the south, Kao-Shi Mountain is to be found. Upon this there are many gems and below it, many sharp stones. [From these they are able to make smooth lancets to cure boils and swellings.] Chu-Shing River is found here, a stream flowing easterly into a marsh, and in it there are many gems and much gold.

8. Three hundred li to the south, Yoh (Lofty) Mountain is found. Upon this there are many mulberry trees and below it many ailantus trees. Loh River is found here, a stream flowing easterly into a marsh, and in it there are many gems and much gold.

9. Three hundred li to the south, Wolf Mountain is to be found. Upon this there is no grass and there are no trees. Below it there is much water (many streams), in which there are many Kan Tsz' fish. [These are not fully described.] They have wild animals, which look like the (quadrumana, called) Kw'a-Fu, but they have hair like that of swine, and their voice is like an expiration of the breath. When these are seen, then heaven sends down great rains.

10. Three hundred li to the South, Lone Mountain is found. Upon this there are many gems and much gold, and below it many beautiful stones. Moh-T'u (Muddy) River is found here, a stream flowing southeasterly into a mighty flood, in which there are many T'iao-Yung. These look like

yellow serpents with fishes fins. They go out and in. They are bright (or smooth). When these are seen the region is subject to great drought.

11. Three hundred li to the south, T'ai (Bald) Mountain is found. [Then the mountain was called the Eastern Yoh or T'ai-Tsung which is now called T'ai Mountain. It is in the northwestern part of Fung-Kao District, and the distance from the foot of the mountain to its summit is forty-eight li and three hundred paces.] Upon this there are many gems, and below it there is much gold. Wild animals are found here which look like sucking pigs, but they have pearls. They are called Tung-Tung, their name being given in imitation of their cry. The Hwan River is found here, a stream flowing easterly into a river. [One authority says that it flows into the sea.] In this there are many water-gems (quartz crystals).

12. Three hundred li to the south, Bamboo Mountain is found bordering on a river. [One authority says that it is on the shore—or that it is at the boundary line.] There is no grass or trees, but there are many green-jasper and green-jade stones. The Kih River (or water impeded in its course by rocks) is found here, a stream flowing southeasterly into Ts'u-Tan River (or a body of water). In this (country) there is a great abundance of dye-plants.

13. The first section of the *Classic of the Eastern Mountains* thus gives the entire distance along the twelve mountains from Suh-Chu Mountain to Bamboo Mountain as three thousand six hundred li. Their gods all have human bodies and dragons' heads.[4] When they are offered a sacrifice of animals having hair, a dog is used. In other sacrifices the blood of a fish is used to besmear the things offered. [To use blood in besmearing the things offered in sacrifice is called "Ni." Kung-Yang's *Chronicles* say that in offering sacrifices having flesh and blood, to the god of the land, and of grain, they besmear with blood the being that is sacrificed. The name of this species of sacrifice is pronounced "Ni."]

Second Section of
Book Four of the *Shan Hai Jing*
Vining's Translation

1. The beginning of the second section of the *Eastern Classic* says that K'ung-Sang Mountain (the Mountain of the Empty Mulberry Trees) on the northern side adjoins the Shih River. [This mountain rises from the Kin-Seh Forest—see the book called *Cheu-Li*.] On the eastern side (it adjoins the states of) Tsu and Wu; on the southern side a number of sandy mounds,

and on the western side the Min (or Muddy) Marsh. Here there are wild animals which look like cattle, but which are striped like tigers. Their voices resemble the sound of a person stretching and yawning. (Perhaps rather the sound of moans.) These are named Ling-Ling, an imitation of their cry. When these are seen, then heaven sends down great rains.

2. Six hundred li to the south, Ts'ao-Chi Mountain is found. Below this there are many paper-mulberry trees, but there is no water (or river). There are many birds and wild animals.

3. Four hundred li to the southwest, Yih-Kao Mountain is found. Upon this there are many gems and much gold, and below it there is much white plaster-rock. The Yih-Kao River is found here, a stream flowing easterly to the Kih-Nu River. In this there are many clams with pearly shells. [These are clams or mussels with shells as beautiful as gems, these pearly shells belonging to a species of mussel called Shan-Pan.]

4. Going to the south, five hundred li by water and three hundred li over shifting sands, one end of the Koh (or Bean) Mountain is reached. There is no grass and there are no trees here, but there are many smooth whetstones.

5. Three hundred and eighty li to the south, the other end of Bean Mountain is found. There is no grass and there are no trees here. The Li River is found here, a stream flowing easterly into the Yu Marsh. In it there are many Chu-P'ieh fish (or water animals). These look like lungs, but have eyes and six feet, and they have pearls. They taste sour, but pleasant, and are eaten without producing sickness. [They do not cause diseases at any time. Lu-Shi's edition of the book of Confucius, called *Spring and Autumn*, says that the Li River contains fish called Chu-Pieh, which have six feet, and which are beautiful as the "vermilion" fish.]

6. Three hundred and eighty li to the south, Yu-Ngo Mountain (or an excessively high peak) is found. Upon this there are many japonica-trees and Jan-trees, and below it there is much prickly succory. The Tsah-Yu River is found here, a stream flowing easterly into the Yellow River. Here there are wild beasts which look like rabbits, but which have a crow's bill, and owl's eyes and a serpent's tail. When they see a man, they pretend to sleep. They are called Chiu-Yu, this sound being an imitation of their cry. When these are seen, grasshoppers of locusts cause great destruction. [Grasshoppers are a species of locusts. It says that they ruin the herbage. Their name is pronounced Chung.]

7. Three hundred li to the south, Tu-Fu Mountain is found. There is no grass and there are no trees here, but there is much water (or there are many streams).

8. Three hundred li to the south, Kang Mountain is found. There is no grass and there are no trees here, but there is much water, and there are many green-jade stones (or there are many water-jade stones). [These are a species of water-gems- i.e. rock crystals.] There are many great serpents, and there are also wild beasts which look like foxes, but which have fish's fins. These are named Chu-Ju, and derive their name from their cry. When these are seen, the country has reason to fear disasters.

9. Three hundred li to the south, Lu-K'i Mountain is found. There is no vegetation, and there are no trees, but there are many stones and much sand. The Sand River is found here, a stream flowing southerly into the Ch'an River (or into a limpid river). In this there are many Li pelicans; these look like ducks, but have men's legs. They derive their name from their cry. When these are seen, then the country will see great literary achievements. [These pelicans have long legs, which somewhat resemble human shanks.]

10. Three hundred and eighty li to the south, Ku-She Mountain is found. There is no grass and there are no trees there, but there is much water (or there are many streams).

11. Going to the south three hundred li by water, and one hundred li over shifting sand, the northern Ku-She Mountain is found. There is no grass and there are no trees, but there are many stones.

12. Three hundred li to the south, Southern Ku-She Mountain is found. There is no grass and there are no trees there, but there is much water (or there are many streams).

13. Three hundred li to the south, Green-jade-stone Mountain is found. There is no grass here but there are many trees. Many great serpents are found here, and there are also many green-jade stones and quartz crystals.

14. Five hundred li to the south, W'ei-Shi Mountain is found. There is no grass there and no trees, but there are many gems and much gold. Yuen River is found here, a stream flowing easterly into Sand Marsh (or into

a sandy marsh). [One authority states that the name of the mountain is pronounced Kiah-Shi instead of W'ei-Shi.]

15. Three hundred li to the south, Ku-Fung Mountain is found. There is no grass, and there are no trees here, but there are many gems and much gold. Wild beasts are found here which look like foxes, but which have wings (or fins). Their voice sounds like that of a wild goose, and they are called Pi-Pi. When these are seen, then heaven sends down great drought.

16. Five hundred li to the south, Fu-Li Mountain is found. Upon this there are many gems and much gold, and below it, many lancet-stones. They have wild beasts which look like foxes, but which have nine tails and nine heads, and tiger's claws. They are called Lung-Chih. Their voice is like that of an infant child, and they eat men.

17. Five hundred li to the south, Yin Mountain is found. To the south, the Yin River is to be seen, and to the north the Hu Marsh (or lakes and marshes). Here they have wild beasts which look like horses, but they have sheep's eyes, four horns and cattle tails. Their voice is like the howl of a dog, and they are called Yiu-Yiu. When these are seen, the country will be visited by many crafty foreigners.[5] They have birds which look like ducks, but they have rats' tails and can climb trees. They are called Chie-Keu. When these are seen, the country will have much sickness.

18. The second section of the *Classic of the Eastern Mountains* thus gives the entire distance along the seventeen mountains, from K'ung-Sang Mountain to Yin Mountain, as six thousand six hundred and forty li. Their gods all have wild beast's bodies but human faces. They bear the Koh fish. (With a species of stag's or deer's horns they catch the Koh fish). When they are offered a sacrifice of living beings having hair or feathers, a fowl is used. When the people pray to them for offspring, they retire to a screened place.

Third Section of
Book Four of the *Shan Hai Jing*
Vining's Translation

1. The beginning of the third section of the *Eastern Classic* says that Shi-Hu Mountain on the north adjoins Siang Mountain. Upon it there are many gems and much gold, and below it there are many thorny plants. There are wild beasts which look like elks, but which have fish eyes, and they are called Wan-Hu (or Yuen-Hu) deriving their name from their cry.

2. Going to the south by water for eight hundred li, K'I Mountain is found (or a mountain with two peaks). Upon this there are many peach-trees and plum-trees. There are also many wild beasts and many tigers.

3. Going to the south by water for five hundred li, Chu-Keu Mountain is found. There are no trees or grass here, but there are many stones, and much sand. The distance around the mountain is one hundred li. There are many Mei (or sleeping) fish here. [These Mei fish are of excellent flavor.]

4. Going south by water for seven hundred li, Middle Fu Mountain is found. Here there are no trees or grass, but there is much sand.

5. Going to the east by water for one thousand li, Hu-She Mountain is found. Here there are no trees or grass, but there are many stones and much sand.

6. Going to the south by water for seven hundred li, Mang-Tsz' (the Eldest Child) is found. Here there are many trees: japonicas and T'ong trees, and also many peach trees and plum trees. In the grass there are many mushroom-rushes (or mushroom and rushes, or Kiun rushes). [These are not fully described. They are called Kw'un.] They have wild beasts, and many elk and deer. The distance around the mountain is one hundred li. Upon it there is a flowing stream called Pih-Yang (or the river of Clear Jade-stone). In this there are many sturgeons and mud-sturgeons. [These mud-sturgeons are a species of eel. They resemble sturgeons, but have a long body like an eel. One authority says that they are a species of herring.]

7. Going south by water for five hundred li, and over shifting sand for five hundred li, a mountain is reached which is called K'I-Chung Mountain, the distance around which is two hundred li. There is no grass and there are no trees here, but there are great serpents, and upon the mountain there are many precious stones. It has a body of water, the distance around which is forty li, all bubbling up and running off. [Now, to the east of the Yellow River is the Fan River, and in the Yin (Dark) District it has the Fun River's Spring (or source). In this place the water rushes out, (over-flowing, bubbling up, and running rapidly. It is deep and cannot be restrained. This is of the same class as the water above referred to.] This is called Shan-Tseh (or the Deep Marsh). In it there are great tortoises. [They have beaks like the common tortoise, the tortoise being a great turtle; the shell has variegated marks, like those of the precious tortoise-shell,

but it is thinner.] Here there are fish (or water animals) which look like carp, which have six feet and a bird's tail. These are called Koh-Koh fish, deriving this name from an imitation of their cry.

8. Going to the south by water for eight hundred li, Mei-Yu Mountain (or Min-Tsz') Mountain is reached. Upon this there are many trees and much grass, and an abundance of gold and gems, and also much ocher. Here there are wild beasts which look like little cattle, but which have horse's tails, and which are called Tsing-Tsing, deriving their name from an imitation of their cry.

9. Going to the south by water for five hundred li, and over shifting sand for three hundred li, Wu-Kao (or Not Lofty) Mountain is reached. Here the Yiu (Young) Sea may be seen. [This is now called the 'Little Sea."] To the east the Fu-tree may be seen [or Fu Sang]. There is no grass and there are no trees here and much wind is found upon the mountain. The distance around it is a hundred li.

10. The third section of the *Eastern Classic* thus gives the entire distance along the nine mountains, for Shi-Hu Mountain to Wu-Kao Mountain, as six thousand eight hundred li. Their gods all have human bodies and sheep's horns. When a sacrifice is offered to them, a ram is used. They use millet for food.[6] When these gods are seen, then wind, rain, and floods cause ruin.

Fourth Section of
Book Four of the *Shan Hai Jing*
Vining's Translation

1. The beginning of the fourth section of the *Eastern Classic* says that the Northern Hao Mountain slopes down to the North Sea. It has trees which look like aspens, but which have red flowers. The fruit is like the jujube, but it has no pit. It tastes sour, but delicious. It is eaten without causing any ill results. The Shih River (or drinkable water) is found here, a stream that flows northeasterly into the sea. Here there are wild animals which look like wolves, but which have red heads and rat's eyes. Their voices sound like those of sucking pigs, and they are called Hieh-Tsu. They eat men. There are birds here which look like domestic fowls, but have white heads, rat's legs, and tiger's claws. They are called Kwei (or K'I) birds, and they eat men.

2. Three hundred li to the south, Mao Mountain is found. Here there are no trees and no grass. The Ts'ang-T'i River is found here, a stream flowing westerly into the Chen River (or into an extensive body of water). In this are many Siu fish. [These are shrimps, or the eels indicated by the character Ts'iu, and possibly the character Siu was then pronounced the same as Ts'iu.]. These look like the carp but have a larger head. Those who eat them have no swellings.

3. Three hundred and twenty li to the south, the Eastern Shi Mountain is found. Upon this there are many green gems. Here there are trees which look like aspens, but which have red veins. Their sap is like blood, and they have no fruit. These are called K'I. They can break horses by its use (i.e. rubbing them with this sap, horses become tame and gentle.)[7] Clear River is found here, a stream flowing northeasterly into the sea. In this there are many delicious cowries and many cuttlefish. These look like a goby, and have only one head with ten bodies. They smell like sedge-grass or a jungle. Those who eat them have no asthma. [It says that they cure the disease which consists of a difficulty in breathing.]

4. Three hundred li to the southeast, Nu-Ching Mountain is found. Upon this there are no trees, grass, or stones. Kao (Rich, Fertilizing) River is found here, a stream flowing westerly into Lih (Cauldron) River.[8] In this there are many thin fish which look like herring, but have only one eye. Their voice sounds like vomiting [i.e. like the sound of a man retching and vomiting]. When these are seen, then heaven sends down a great drought.

5. Two hundred li to the southeast, the K'in (Imperial or Majestic) Mountain is found. Here there are many gems and much gold, but no stones. The Shi River is found there, a stream flowing northerly into Kao marsh. In this there are many eels and cowrie-shells. Here there are wild animals which look like sucking pigs, but which have tusks. These are called Tang K'ang, deriving their name from their cry. When these are seen, then heaven causes the earth to produce much grain.

6. Two hundred li to the southeast, Tsz'-T'ung Mountain is found. Tsz'-T'ung River is found here, a stream flowing westerly into Yu-Ju Marsh. In this there are many Hwah fish. These look like fish, but have bird's wings. They go out and in. They are bright. Their voices sound like those of the Yuen-Yang. When these are seen, then heaven sends down a great drought.

7. Two hundred li to the northeast, Yen (Sharp-pointed) Mountain is found; there are many precious stones and much gold. There are also wild beasts which look like swine, but which have men's faces and yellow bodies, but red tails. They are called Hoh-Yu. Their voices sound like that of an infant child. These wild animals eat men, and eat vermin and serpents. When these are seen, then heaven sends down great rains.

8. Two hundred li to the east, T'ai (Immense) Mountain is found. Upon it there are many precious stones and much gold, and there are also many wax-trees. [These wax-trees do not shed their leaves in winter.] Here there are many wild animals which look like cattle, but which have a white head, one eye, and a serpent's tail. They are called Fei. When they go upon the water, they dry it up, and when they go upon the grass, they kill it. When these are seen, then heaven sends down a great pestilence. (Its body is full of a poisonous principle. The book called *K'i-Kin* says that is a locust or cricket called K'iung. Its body looks harmless, but it causes the veins to wither and dry up being more poisonous than the Chan. All creatures fear it, and wish to keep at a great distance from it.) The Keu River is found here, a stream flowing northerly into Lao River. In this are many fish.

9. The fourth section of the *Eastern Classic* thus gives the entire distance along the eight mountains, from Hao Mountain to T'ai Mountain, as one thousand seven hundred and twenty li.

10. The above record of the *Classic of the Eastern Mountains* thus gives the distance along these forty-six mountains as eighteen thousand eight hundred and sixty li.[9]

Author's Note

Now we come to the all-important Record of the Ninth and Fourteenth Books of the *Shan Hai Jing*. This is human history at its most dramatic point. Here tribes and nations are presented before our admiring and astonished gaze. We see the Chinese leaders in the New World, of the post-deluvian epoch, leading their children in rites. We hear of the gods of the Fu Sang people, or rather, the images which were set up so they would remember their fathers.

Would we not have enjoyed being with Ti Tsun on that lovely day at the Grand Canyon when he condescended to be the friend of the "variegated birds" in all their finery! What a spectacle, when he descended with them two terraces deep, into the gorgeous glories of the place where the sun was born, and there led the worship! Emperor Shun had owned the high places of the terraces, but the birds controlled them.[10]

In the Ninth Book we view the nations from the delectable heights of Cha Hill at the place where Mexico City was later found. We witness the antics of the "Giants" of Lower California, admire the "Refined Gentlemen" of California and the silk-clad citizens of the Green Hills. It was there that the fearless Shu-Hai took his abacus and pointed north of the Green Hills, and began pacing out the distances of Fu Sang. After all, it was Emperor Yao who had commanded Shu-Hai to make the American survey … and so he was determined to obey the ruler, or perish.

There are many interesting folk: the Naked People, the Black Teeth Tribe, and the Black People. She-Pi's concubine was in the north, and her lover wore snakes in his ears. The people with the charming black hips had sea gulls for fishing companions. The Hairy People are unusual, but the Distressed People had their problems. The square-faced wood eaters were the most "different" dieters of the whole district. Read for yourself the strange thing of primeval Fu Sang.

Ninth Book of the *Shan Hai Jing*
Vining's Translation

The *Classic of the Regions Beyond the Eastern Sea*, in regard to the regions beyond the sea, from its southeast corner to its northeast corner.

1. The Cha Hill [Pronounced Cha or perhaps Fah.] It is said that this country produces I gems, green horses,[11] Shi-Juh, common willows, delicious cherries, sweet flowers, and excellent fruits. It is in the Easter Sea between two mountains. Upon the hill there are lofty trees.[12] One authority says that its name is Cha-Kiu, and one says that the Country of a Hundred Fruits lies east of Yao's burial place.[13]

2. The Great Men's Country is north of this. Because the men are great they sit and seize passing boats. One authority says that this country is north of Cha-Kiu.

3. She-Pi's Body is north of this. [This is the name of a god.] He has a wild animal's body and a man's face. He has large ears, and for ear-ornaments, has two green serpents [i.e., he has ear-ornaments like serpents strung in his ears.] One authority says that Kan-Yu's Body lies north of the Great Men's Country.

4. The Country of Refined Gentlemen lies north of this. They have clothing, caps, sashes and swords. They eat wild beasts, and have two great tigers, one on each side. They are very gentle and do not quarrel. They have fragrant plants. [Perhaps "clay" should be read instead of "fragrant plants."] They have a flowering-plant which produces blossoms in the morning which die in the evening. One authority says that it is north of Kan-Yu's Body.

5. Hung-Hung lies north of this. They all have two heads. [The name is pronounced the same as that of the character Hung, which means rainbow.] One authority says that it is north of the Country of the Refined Gentlemen.

6. The god of the Valley of the Dawn (Chao-Yang) is called Tien-Wu. He is the god of the water. He dwells north of Hung-Hung between two bodies of water. When he appears as a wild animal, he has eight heads with human faces, eight legs, and eight tails, and is all green and yellow. [The "Classic of the Great Eastern Waste" says he has ten tails.][14]

7. The Green Hills Country is situated north of this. [The people eat all kinds of grain, and have silken clothing.][15] Here there are foxes with four legs and eight tails. One authority says this is situated north of the "Manifestation of the Dawn." [Kih-Kiun's *Bamboo Book* says that P'oh-Shu-Tsz' went on a military expedition in the eastern sea for fully three years, and found a fox with nine tails, which, perhaps, was a species of the fox above described.]

8. The sovereign ordered Shu-Hai to walk from the farthest limit of the East to the farthest limit of the West, five hundred thousand and ten times ten thousand paces [Shu-Hai was a dauntless traveler] and nine thousand eight hundred paces. Shu-Hai grasped an abacus in his right hand and with his left hand he pointed to the north of the Beautiful Green Hills. One authority says that it was the Emperor Yu who commanded Shu-Hai: one says that the distance was five hundred thousand, ten times ten thousand, nine thousand and eight hundred paces. [The poem "Ts'ang-Shan-Wu" says that heaven and earth, from east to west, are three- hundred and thirty- three thousand li, and from south to north, two- hundred and one thousand five-hundred li. To inspect heaven and earth, go one hundred fifty thousand li.][16]

9. The Black-Teeth Country lies north of this. [The *History of the Eastern Barbarians* says that forty li east of Japan there is a country called the

Naked People's Country, and that southeast of this lies the Black Teeth Country. A ship can reach it by sailing for one year. The *Account of Strange Things* says that the Western Butchers dye their teeth and are like these people.] The people are black, and eat rice.[17] They also eat serpents, some red and some green [One authority mentions only the green serpents.] It is very great. One authority says that it is north of (the country of) Shu-Hai.[18] and has people with black hands who eat rice, and who use serpents, one serpent being red. Below it is the Warm Springs (T'ang) Ravine. [In the ravine there is hot water.] Above Warm Springs Ravine is Fu Sang [i.e., the Fu Sang tree, or the useful mulberry-tree.] The place where the ten suns bathe lies north of the Black-Teeth (Country). In the water there is a large tree having nine suns in its lower branches and one sun in its upper branches. (Chwang-Cheu says that formerly these ten suns rose all together, and grass and trees were burned and withered. Hwai-Nan-Tz' says that (the emperor) Yao then commanded (the prince) Y to shoot nine of the ten suns, and the bird in the suns, until dead.

The "Dissipation of Sorrows" says in reference to it that Y brought the sun-bird to an end, and that it dropped some of its feathers, and that Y took them home and kept them. *The Ching-Mu Classic* says that formerly this Y shot skillfully, and brought these ten suns to an end. Kih-Kiun's *Bamboo Book* says that when Yin-Kiah ascended to the throne and dwelt at Si-Ho there were strange prodigies. Ten suns rose and shone together. This is a wonder of nature, but there is proof of it. Tradition says that there were ten suns in the sky, the number of suns being ten. This account says that nine of the suns dwell in the lower branches and one sun in the upper branches.[19] The *Classic of the Great Waste* says that when one sun sets, another sun rises and lights heaven and earth, and although there are ten suns, they rise alternately, and so revolve and shine; but at the time referred to they all rose together, and so heaven sent down supernatural calamities.

Therefore, Y, having asked for Yao's instructions, and thoroughly understanding his heart's desire, looked up to heaven, and pulled the bowstring, and nine suns retired and concealed themselves.... If we examine into this in a common-sense way we find that it is not reasonable, but if we investigate the principles of destiny we find that nothing is impossible. You who stand by and see ought to try and comprehend this mystery. Those things which relate to the mysterious and obscure are hard to understand, but nevertheless they go on their course without obstruction. Yu-Shi's Concubine dwells north of this. [Yu-Shi is the same as P'ing-I, the God of Rain.] He, as a man, is black, and in each of his hands he holds a serpent. In his left ear there is a green serpent, and in his right ear a red serpent. One authority says that he dwells north of (the country of) the Ten Suns, that as a man he has a black body and a human face, and that each (hand) holds a tortoise.

10. The Black-Hip Country lies north of this. [So called because the people are all black below the waist.] These people make clothing from water animals or fish [i.e., they make clothing from the skins of fish-or water animals.][20] They eat gulls. [Gulls are water birds. Their name is pronounced Yiu.] They use two birds, carrying them in their arms. One authority says that this lies north of Yu-Shi's concubine.

11. The Hairy People's Country lies north of this, and has people upon whose bodies hair grows. (At the present time, by leaving the region of the Lin Sea, and going two thousand li to the southeast, the place of residence of the hairy people is found upon the Great Loh Island.) Upon this island there are people with short, small faces and with their bodies entirely covered with hair, like a hog or moose. They live in caves, and have no clothing or garments. [In the reign of the Ts'in Dynasty in the fourth year of the period distinguished by the appellation Yung-Kai (or "Perpetual Excellence" i.e. in the year 310 A.D.) an officer named Tai, having charge of the salt at Wu-Kien, found upon the seashore a boat containing men and women, four people in all. These all looked alike and spoke a language which was not intelligible. They were sent to the prime minister's palace, but before they had reached it they all died on the way, except only one. The ruler gave him a wife, who bore children to him. Going to and coming from the market and wells, he advanced slowly in acquiring the language. His native place was the Hairy People's Country. The *Classic of the Great Waste* says that the Hairy Tribe eat a species of millet for food.] One authority says that this country is north of the Black-Hip Country.

12. The Distressed (Lao) People's Country lies north of this. It has people who are black [and who for food eat the fruits of trees and plants: they have a bird with two heads.] Perhaps the name should be read the "Kiao People," instead of the Distressed (or Lao) People. One authority says that it lies north of the Hairy People and has people having their faces, eyes, hands, and feet entirely black.[21]

13. The K'eu-Wang of the Eastern Regions has a bird's body, a human face, and he rides upon two dragons. [He is the God of Wood, and has a square face, and wears plain apparel. Moh-Tsz says that formerly, in the Ts'in

Dynasty, Muh-Kung was of illustrious virtue. The Supreme Ruler caused K'eu-Wang to lengthen his life by nineteen years.]

Fourteenth Book of the *Shan Hai Jing*
Vining's Translation

1. "The Great Canyon Beyond the Eastern Seas" (the poem called "Ts'ang-Shan-Wu" says that in the east there is a stream flowing in a bottomless ravine. It is supposed to be this canyon. The "Dissipation of Sorrows" calls it Kiang-Shang's Great Canyon) in Shao-Hao's Country. [The Emperor Shao-Hao, of the "Golden Heaven" family, gave it this designation.] Shao-Hao's Descendant, the Emperor Chwen-Suh (of whom no further description is given), left there his lute and lyre. (It says that his lute and lyre are in this canyon). It has a beautiful mountain, from which there flows a delightful spring, producing a charming gulf. [The water accumulates and so forms a gulf.]

2. In the southeastern corner of the Great Eastern Waste there is a mountain called the Pi-Mu-Ti Hill.

3. In the Great Waste beyond the Eastern Sea there is a mountain which by hyperbole is called[22] "The Place where the Sun and Moon Rise." It has rolling valleys and mountains. This is the Great Men's Country. [In the Ts'in Dynasty, in the second year of the period distinguished by the designation Yung-Kia ("Perpetual Excellence," i.e., in 308 A.D.), there were ducks collected in Ngao-Po, twenty li south of the district of Shi-Ngan. A man by the name of Cheu-Fu-Chang picked up a wooden arrow with an iron point, which was six feet and a half long. Reckoning from the length of the arrow, the shooter much have been a rod and five or six feet tall. The Coreans say that formerly[23] some people from the kingdom of Japan, who encountered bad weather upon a voyage, were blown across the "Great Sea," and beyond it they discovered a country where the people were all a rod tall and moreover, in their form and appearance, they looked like Mongols. They were tall savages of a foreign tribe. The arrow came from this country. The Wai-Chwen says that the shortest of the Scorched Pigmy People were only three feet high, and the tallest of these did not exceed ten rods. In Ho-Tu's *Album of Gems* it is said that ninety thousand li north of the Kwun-Lun (Range of Mountains) the Lung-Poh Country is found, where the people are thirty rods tall, and live for eighteen thousand years, but then they die. East of the Kwun-Lun (Mountains) Ta-Tsin is found. The people are ten rods tall, and all wear plain garments. Ten times ten thousand li to the east, the country of the

T'iao People is found. They are thirty rods and five feet tall. East of this, ten times ten thousand li, is the central Tsin Country, whose people are one rod tall. *The Kuh-Liang History* says that the body of a tall savage, measured crosswise, covered nine Chinese acres. When riding, his head and shoulders reached above the cross-bar of the chariot. This man must therefore have been several rods tall. In the time of the Ts'in Dynasty a giant was seen in Lin-T'ao who was five rods tall, and his foot-prints were six feet long. If the above accounts can be considered to be true, then there is no limit to the height of these tall men.] It has the Great Men's Market, which is called the "Great Men's Mansion." [This is a mountain which is so named because of its resemblance to a large mansion. The Great Men collect near it at market-times, and hold a market upon and about it.] It has a great man crouching upon both of its sides. [Perhaps the character translated "crouching" formerly meant "sitting erect." Chwang-Tsz' says that he sat in Hwui-K'iai.] It has a country of "Little People" who are called the Tsing People. [The poem called Ts'ang-Shan-Wu says that the farthest region to the northeast is inhabited by people who are only nine inches tall.] Its god has a human face and a wild beast's body, and he is called Li-Ling's Body.

4. There is also a mountain name Kueh, from which the Aspen River flows.

5. There is also a Country of Plants, where millet is used for food.[24] [It says that millet grows in this country. The name of the country is pronounced Wei.] They employ (or have) four (species of) birds (i.e., they have numerous varieties of birds); also, tigers, panthers, brown bears and grizzly bears.[25]

6. In the Great Waste there is a mountain called Hoh-Hu. It is the place where the sun and moon rise. It has Chung-Yung's Country. Ti-Tsun (or the Emperor Tsun) begat Chung-Yung. The people of Chung-Yung eat wild beasts and the fruits of trees. [In this country there are red trees with dark wood, which have delicious flowers and fruit. See Lu-Shi's edition of the work of Confucius called *Spring and Autumn*.] They use four birds (i.e., they have numerous species of birds), and also panthers, tigers, brown bears and grizzly bears.

7. There is also the Mountain of the Eastern Pass, and here is the "Country of Refined Gentlemen." These people have clothing, caps, sashes and swords. [They have tigers and panthers, which are gentle and give Way.)] Here is the Country of Presiding Spirits. Ti-Tsun begat Yen-Lung who

begat the Presiding Spirits. The Presiding Spirits have off-spring but the pure minded male has no wife, and the pure-minded female has no husband. [It says that these people are pure in their thoughts and are not affected by passion and do not mate, but that they conceive children with all purity, like white doves looking steadfastly into each other's eyes, each being affected by the purity of the other.] [26] They eat millet and wild beasts, and have numerous varieties of birds. Here is Ta-O Mountain (or the Mountain of the Great Ridge).

8. In the Great Waste there is a mountain named Ming-Sing (or the Bright Star). It is the place where the sun and moon rise.

9. There is also the White People's Country. Ti-Tsun begat Ti-Hung, who begat the White People. The White People have no surnames. They eat millet, and have numerous varieties of birds, as well as tigers, panthers, brown bears and grizzly bears. [And they have teams of yellow wild beasts, which they drive, using them in order to reach a great age.]

10. There is also the Green Hills Country. Here there are foxes with nine tails. [When they are disturbed they come out of their holes, and this is considered a very good omen.] It has the Jeu-Puh (Courteous Vassal) Country. They live in a country of luxuriant land. [It is as luxuriant as if irrigated. The name is pronounced Ying.] It has the country of Black Teeth. (Their teeth are like lacquer.) Ti-Tsun begat the Black Teeth. [As the teachings and examples of the sage do not reach all regions, therefore in after ages his descendants differ in their pursuits and outward appearance. Every one says that those who are now living are his descendants: but they surely cannot be posterity which he himself begat.] The Kiang tribe eat millet for food, and have numerous varieties of birds. Here is also the Hia-Cheu (Summer Island) Country. Here is a also the Kai-Yu Country. It has a god with eight heads with human faces, and tiger's body and ten tails. He is called T'ien-wu. [He is the God of the Water.]

11. In the Great Waste there is a mountain called Kuh-Ling-Yu-T'ien. It is at the farthest limit of the east with Li and Meu. [These are the names of three mountains.] At the place where the sun and moon rise [there is a god] called Cheh-Tan. In the Eastern Region he is called Cheh. The "coming wind" is called Chan. [It is not fully described where the place of the Coming Wind is situated.] He dwells at the farthest limit of the east, and produces the eight winds. [It says that this man is able to regulate the proper times for the winds to come forth and return.]

12. In an island of the Eastern Sea there is a god with a human face and a bird's body, having two yellow serpents for ear-ornaments. [These serpents are passed through his ears.] He treads upon two yellow serpents, and is called Yu-Kwoh. Hwang-Ti begat Yu-Kwoh, and begat Yu-King.[27] [Yu-King is the same as Yu-Kiang.] Yu-King dwells in the North Sea, and Yu-Kwoh dwells in the Eastern Sea. They are sea gods. [They are each called the god of that particular sea over which they rule.[28] One original authority reads Hao instead of Kwoh.]

13. There is also the Chao-Yao (Quaking) Mountain, where the Yung (Melting) River flows. Here there is a country called the Black-Hip Country. [From the hips down they are black like lacquer]. They have millet for food, and have numerous varieties of birds. Here is also the country of the Kw'un (Needy) People, whose surname is Keu, who eat birds. Some say that King Hai held a bird in his two hands, and when he had eaten its head, King Hai sent it to Yiu-I, Ho-Poh, and Puh-Niu (Ho-Poh and Puh-Niu are both names and surnames—see Kih-Kiun's *Bamboo Book*.) Yiu-I slew King Hai, and captured Puh-Niu. [The *Bamboo Book* says that Hai, the son of the Emperor Yin, went as a visitor to the house of Yui-I, and committed adultery there. Therefore, Yiu-I's sovereign, Min-Ch'an, slew him, and thus made an example of him. Therefore the Emperor Yin-Kieh-Ching borrowed troops of Ho-Poh, with which to punish Yiu-I, overthrow his country, and slay his sovereign Min-Ch'an.] Ho pitied Yiu-I[29], and allowed him to leave the country secretly and go to a region of wild beasts; and because he ate the wild beasts, he was called a Yao man. [Yiu-I was originally a friend of Ho-Poh, and a good scholar; but because Kieh-Ching, who was then the emperor of the Ying Country, had a good and rightful reason for borrowing troops to punish crime, Ho-Poh could not do otherwise than to help overthrow his country. It was because he pitied Yiu-I that he allowed him to leave the country secretly. After he had left he became a Yao man.] The sovereign Shun begat Hi, and Hi begat the Yao (Quaking) People.[30] In the sea there are two people. [These are the people to whom Yiu-I went.] They are called Nu-Cheu. [They are the same as Nu-Cheu's Body. There is no certainty as to the time when, or the kind of being into which she (Nu-Cheu's Body) may be metamorphosed; for at one time she walks on water, and at another she vanishes into earth. There is no place she could not reach if she desired to reach it. We hear also that the ways of the class of Fan Lis are similar to those of Nu-Cheu's Body.][31] Nu-Cheu has great crabs. The breadth is ten li.

14. In the Great Waste there is a mountain called Yeh-Yao-Kiun-Ti. Upon it is the Fu-tree, having a trunk three hundred li. Its leaves are like mustard.

[It resembles a pillar rising to a great height, and its leaves are like mustard greens.] It has a valley called the Warm Spring Valley. Above the Warm Springs Valley is the Fu-tree [i.e. Fu Sang lies above.] When one sun sets another sun rises. [It says that they alternate with each other.] They all contain a bird. [In them there is a two-footed bird.] Here there is a god with a human face, dog's ears, and a wild beast's body. For ear ornaments he has two green serpents. He is called She-Pi's Body. They have birds variegated with all colors. Ti-Tsun condescended to be their friend. Ti descended two high terraces (for worship) which were ruled by the variegated birds. [It says that below the mountain were Shun's two high terraces for worship, and that the variegated birds ruled over them.]

15. In the Great Waste there is a mountain called I-T'ien-Su-Man. It is the place where the sun and moon were born, and here is the Huen (a pipe, a musical instrument) People's Country. Here is also the K'i (Dark Gray) Mountain, the Yao (Quaking) Mountain, the Tsang Mountain, the Man-Hu (or Household) Mountain, the Shing (Fertile) Mountain, and the Tai Mountain. Here there are variegated birds.

16. In the Eastern Waste there is a mountain called Hoh-Ming-Tsun-Tsih. This is the place where the sun and moon rise. There is also the Kih-Yung Country, northeast beyond the sea. They had three blue (or green) horses, and three horses that were black with white spots, sweet flowers, Yuen-Yiu, I gems, three green (or blue) horses, and three black horses with white spots like eyes[32] on their flesh, sweet flowers, delicious cherries, and numerous varieties of grain in this place. [It says that these are produced spontaneously.]

17. There is also the country of Nu-Hwo-Yueh-Mu, having a man called Yuen. In the northern regions they say that Yuen, who brings them the wind, is called Yen. [It says that he has these two names.] He dwelt at the extreme eastern corner, for the sun and moon dwelt there. They did not have a uniform time for rising and setting, and he controlled them as to whether the time should be short or long. [It says that Yuen had the management of the observations of the rising and setting of the sun and moon. He did not let them run out of order, and he knew the length of the days.][33]

18. In the northeast corner of the Great Waster there is a mountain called Hiung-Li-Ti Hill. The Ying Dragon dwells at its extreme southern limit.[34] [The Ying Dragon is a dragon having wings.] He killed Ch'i- Yiu, together with Kw'a-Fu [Ch'i-yiu was a soldier.] He could not ascend again. [The

Ying Dragon therefore dwells below the earth.] Formerly, when below, he was the occasion of dry weather [then it did not rain above], but when the Ying Dragon made his appearance there was a very great rain. [The dragon that is in heaven was produced by the vapor ascending from the Ying Dragon. This is the work of the mysterious and obscure, and man is not capable of accomplishing it.]

19. In the Eastern Sea is the Mountain (or Island) of the Flowing Stream, seven thousand li distant in the sea. Upon this there are wild beasts which look like cattle, with green (blue or hoary) bodies, but they have no horns, and only one foot. When they come out of or go into the water, then there is wind and rain. They are bright like the sun and moon, and their voice is like thunder. They are called Kw-Ei. The Yellow Emperor obtained them and made drums of their skins, beating them with drumsticks made from the bones of wild beasts. [The Thunder Beast is the God of Thunder. He has a man's face and a dragon's body. He drums his abdomen, beating it with drum sticks.] The sound might be heard for five hundred li, terrifying all beneath heaven.

Vining stated,

> A more careful examination of the original text of the *Shan Hai King* demonstrates beyond question that this "Sacred Book of Geography" contains not only fabulous tales, such as might be expected in a work of such great antiquity, but also precise scientific statements from which the scholarly world can obtain much knowledge of the archaic period of the Chinese monarchy.[5]

Note by Harris: Since Emperor Shun was grandfather of the Yao people, the White people and the Chung Yung people and himself begat the Black Teeth People—he must have come to America! This is made certain by the story of how he condescended to worship with the "Variegated Birds" on the lower terraces of the canyon, which belonged to him.

Back cover of map book 5

End Notes

Chapter 1

[1] Edward Vining, *Inglorious Columbus*, Appleton, 1885, p. 221
[2] Ibid., p. 57, 58
[3] Ibid, p. 217, "D'Hervey's Appendix"
[4] Vining, p. 219
[5] Ibid., p. 220
[6] Henriette Mertz, *Pale Ink,* Chicago, Il., p. 94-96
[7] Ibid., p. 97
[8] Vining, p. 218
[9] We owe thanks to David Hawkes for his sensitive translation of *The Songs of the South*, an ancient Chinese anthology, Oxford, 1957

Chapter 2

[1] Vining, p. 669
[2] Mertz, p. 94-95
[3] Ibid., p. 18
[4] M. Bazin, *Journal Asiatique*, 1839
[5] Bazin on authority of Vining, page 673
[6] Ibid.
[7] A remarkable verification that both Yu and Y went overseas, and afterwards wrote the *Shan Hai Jing*. The testimony, so fully vindicating of the Fu Sang maps, makes the reality of their trip certain and established.
[8] Yong Shun, *Shan Hai Jing*, Ming Dynasty copy
[9] Vining, p. 678
[10] On authority of Joseph Needham, *Clerks and Craftsmen in China and the West*, England: Cambridge University Press, 1970, p. 504

Chapter 3

[1] Vining, p. 9&10
[2] Needham, p. 43
[3] Charles H. Hapgood, *Maps of the Ancient Sea Kings*, Chilton Books, New York, 1966 p. 145
[4] Sih Mah Gwan, *Tz Jih Taeng Jan* (Chou to Tang History) Vol. 176, Taipei, Wen Gwang Bookstore, 1972 (Chen Dynasty Record 10, p. 5494)
[5] Chau Ju Kua, *Chu Fan Chi*, p. 35
[6] Olivia Vlahos, *Indian Cultures in America*, p. 126
[7] Mertz, p. 17
[8] Vining, p. 220
[9] Ibid.
[10] William H. Prescott, *Conquest of Mexico*, p. 63

Chapter 4

[1] Vining, p. 94

[2] The *Odyssey* refers to a long held belief that the Aeolis chief kept a bag of souls in a floating island, thus floating ghosts. Perhaps the Chinese while there heard this myth.

[3] Charles E. Chapman, *A History of California—The Spanish Period*, Macmillan, New York, 1921, p. 21

Chapter 5

[1] De Paravey (on authority of Vining) p. 50-51. Is it not amazing that De Paravey's testimony and that of DeGuiness regarding the Fu Sang Maps has been so long ignored?

[2] De Paravey made a serious error, and thought the name blocks were islands. They referred to places on the "ring-continent" of which the western American coast formed a strategic part!

[3] De Paravey (on authority of Vining) p. 51

[4] Joseph Needham, "Clerks and Craftsmen in China and the West," *Science and Civilization in China*, (Five Volumes), Cambridge University Press, 1970, p. 19

[5] Charles Hapgood, "Maps of the Ancient Sea Kings," Chilton Books, New York, N. Y. 1966, p. 67

[6] Hubert Howe Bancroft, "Works," Vol. 1, History of Northwest Coast, 1884, p.131. The fact that the Englishman and the Frenchman both believed in Fu Sang was a definite spur and encouragement to me.

[7] Hirosi Nakamura,"Old Chinese World Maps Preserved by the Koreans," *Mapa Mundi*, Vol. 4. p. 19

[8] A map of the world. The Korean Repository, Vol. I, 336-341, with 1 plate, 1892

[9] Nakamura, p. 31

[10] Nakamura, p. 10

[11] The more the European side is studied the more we will realize the "common sense" of the Chinese map names. Most of the designations are reasonable.

[12] Ibid., p. 12-13

[13] I am stunned that mighty Nakamura could come so close and not unlock the great doors right in front of him.

[14] Ibid., p. 19

[15] Many names on this listing are from Nakamura's writings

Chapter 6

[1] Edward Vining, p. 9 & 10

[2] Joseph Needham, *Clerks and Crafsmen in China and the West*, Cambridge University Press, Cambridge, England, Vol. III, p. 534

[3] Ibid., p. 535-536

[4] We are indebted, once again to the vast researches of Dr. Needham, for this charming story

[5] Ibid., p. 538

[6] A series of 18 maps, more or less, appears to be typical of ancient map book formats.

[7] Joseph Needham, *Science and Civilization in China* Vol. III, pages 33 and 540

[8] Charles G. Leland, *Fu Sang*, New York: J.W. Bouton, 1875, p. 32

[9] Ibid., p. 89 forward. Note by author: The clumsy nineteenth century translations of Chinese words the reader will please bear with. We dare not try to pronounce them differently, lest we insert wrong words or names!

[10] J.C. Beaglehole, *The Exploration of the Pacific*, London: A. C. Black, Ltd., 1934, p. 70

[11] Article by Otis T. Mason, *Smithsonian Reports*, 1894, p. 535

[12] Ibid.

[13] Hapgood, p. 44 (Robert Thorne's Map)

[14] Ibid., p. 99

[15] Ibid., p. 145

Chapter 7

[1] G.W. James, *In and Around the Grand Canyon*, Boston: Little, Brown, and Co., 1908. p. 331

[2] *The Historical Memoirs of Se-Ma-Tsien* translated by E. Chavannes, 1895 p. 47

[3] James, p. 91

[4] Ibid., p. 330

[5] Ibid., p. 239-241

[6] Ibid., p. 93

[7] Mertz, p.18

Chapter 8

[1] Vining, p. 221

[2] Herbert Joseph Spinden, *Maya Art and Civilization*, Indian Hill, CO, Falcon Wing Press, 1957, Tabular View of Maya Chronology, opposite plate LXV and p. 12

[3] Holy Bible KJV, Matthew 2:1-2 "Now when Jesus was born in Bethlehem of Judea in the days of Herod the king, behold, there came wise men from the east to Jerusalem, saying, Where is he that is born King of the Jews? for we have seen his star in the east, and are come to worship him." Then verse 3 adds "When Herod the king heard these things, he was troubled, and all Jerusalem …" Note these facts: a. These men came from the east. No one can prove China and Fu Sang were not represented. [This story is also in Chinese legend.] b. This delegation had almost supernatural knowledge to come and say what they did. c. Evidently there was a visible new star to confirm the account of these astronomers. The story of the wise men is tied in with the slaughter of the innocents that followed (a historically verifiable event).

[4] Joseph Needham: *Science and Civilization in China*, University of Cambridge, Chinese Reprint, Taipei, 1970, p. 251

[5] Needham, *Clerks and Craftsmen in China and the West*, p. 5

[6] Ibid.

[7] Cyrus Gordon, *Before Columbus*, New York: Crown Publishing, 1971, p. 171
[8] *City of God*, 8:2
[9] Gordon, p. 171
[10] Vining, p. 221

Chapter 9

[1] Needham, *Science and Civilization in China*, Vol. 3, p. 188, First chapter of the Shu Ching (Historical Classic)
[2] Margaret L. Ionides and Stephen A. Ionides, *Stars and Men*, Indianapolis, Indiana: Bobbs-Merrill, 1939, p. 138
[3] Vining, p. 250

Chapter 10

[1] A fenestrated rudder has openings through which water can pass. The fenestrations ease the steering by reducing the pressure against which the tiller has to act, while leaving the efficiency unaffected. This led indirectly to the slotted wing in aircraft.
[2] Needham, *Clerks and Craftsmen in China and the West*, p. 250 forward
[3] Shen Kua on authority of Needham, *Science and Civilization in China*, Vol. III, p. 574-575
[4] Ibid.
[5] Shun Tien, 5
[6] Needham, vol. II, p. 327
[7] Ibid.
[8] Ibid., p. 100

Chapter 11

[1] Vining, "Shorter Essays," p. 165
[2] O. T. Mason, p. 539

Chapter 12

[1] Gordon, p.139 forward.
[2] *The Weekly Colonist*, Victoria, B.C., Wednesday, October 25th, 1882
[3] The name "Dah Ren" means "Big Men," and the original Dahren, or Dairen, was in Alaska.
[4] Vining, p. 246 "Professor Williams' Argument"
[5] *Classic of the Mountains and Seas*, Book 9
[6] *China News*, Taipei, Taiwan, Jan. 14, 1969
[7] Ibid.
[8] Vining, p. 220. It is highly likely Vining is right, and some "Americans" came back to China.
[9] Gordon, p. 204 (These Tibetan maps have fascinating possibilities as proofs).
[10] Mertz, pp. 100-101

Chapter 13

[1] Vining, p. 31

[2] Olivia Vlahos, *Indian Cultures in the Americas*, Greenwich, Conn.: Fawcett Publ. p. 117

[3] Fragment of *Walam Olum*, p. 62, Author unknown.

[4] Mertz, p. 37

[5] *Chu Fan Chi*, p. 169

[6] Alpheus Hyatt Verrill and Ruth Verrill, *America's Ancient Civilizations*, Putnam, New York, 1953, p. 90

[7] William C. Boyd, *Genetics and the Races of Man*, Boston: Little, Brown and Co., 1950

[8] Prescott, p. 702

[9] Vining, p. 706

Chapter 14

[1] William Edward Soothill and Lewis Hodous, Kegan Paul, *A Dictionary of Chinese Buddhist Terms*, Trench, Trubner, and Co., 1970, p. 193

[2] Ibid.

[3] Ibid.

[4] E.T.C. Werner, "A Note on Head-Flattening," *New China Review*, Vol. 1, 1919, p. 19

[5] Ibid.

[6] Ibid.

[7] Ibid.

[8] *Dictionary of Expressions*, Taiwan, 1972, p. 1183

[9] Hui Shan always spoke of going East instead of Northeast.

[10] There can be no question that the Maya leaders were Chinese, even as these maps so plainly imply.

[11] The map plainly calls Yucatan "The Land of Huan Tow;" furthermore, the *Shan Hai Jing* says Yao was buried in that region. I think it highly likely that this is true.

[12] Werner, p. 21

[13] On the authority of Needham, *Science and Civilization in China*, Vol. 1, p. 204

[14] Ibid.

[15] Ibid.

[16] Ibid.

[17] The peculiar "American" need for trepanation was largely due to the types of punishment and of warfare practiced there. Clubs were often deliberately used as means of punishing or rebuking subordinates. Fu Sang soldiers were much more interested in capturing than killing. They wanted slaves and sacrificial victims. So to stun a man was the prime objective. This, of course, resulted in much brain damage, severe head pains, water on the brain, skull fractures, etc. Trepanation might relieve pain or make a dull servant brighten up a bit. Perhaps another blow of the club, just before the operation was a helpful anesthetic!

[18] Victor Von Hagen, *Realm of the Incas*, New York: Mentor Books, 1957, p. 108 and 109

Chapter 15

[1] The shattering terrors of missionary Islam were still two centuries in the future. This was Buddhism's great opportunity, before East and West were cut off from each other.

[2] Mertz, p. 15

[3] Vining, p. 522

About the Author

[1] Hendon M. Harris, Jr., *Laughter and Tears* (a selection of poems), p. 7, Berne, IN.: Light and Hope Publications, 1954

[2] According to *Funk and Wagnalls Encyclopedia* late in the 12th Century a colony of Jews settled in the city. The colonists maintained their racial purity and religious faith for many centuries, but were gradually assimilated through intermarriage." See picture of my grandfather with some of these Jewish Chinese. They even left a written history giving the names of the immigrants.

[3] The accounts of Kaifeng and the Hendon Harris, Sr. family are gathered from *How Beautiful the Feet*, by Florence Powell Harris (mother of Hendon, Jr.), Hong Kong: Suen Shing Printing Co., 1968

[4] Hendon M. Harris, Jr., *The American Idol*, 1961, p. 3

[5] Hendon M. Harris, Jr., *The Asiatic Fathers of America, (The Chinese Discovery and Colonization of America)*, Taipei: Wen Ho Printing Co., Ltd., 1974, p. 167

[6] Ibid.

[7] Hendon M. Harris, Jr., *Laughter and Tears*, Berne, IN., Light and Hope Publishing, 1954, p. 4

[8] Hendon M. Harris, Jr., *Poems for Grown Up Children*, Berne, IN: Light and Hope Publications, p. 2

[9] *Holy Bible*, King James Version, Ephesians 2:8-9

English Translation of Sections of the *Shan Hai Jing*

[1] Vining, *Inglorious Columbus*

[2] Mertz, pp. 110 to 139

[3] The large figures or designs, discernable from planes in South America, may very likely have a connection with the gods and symbols mentioned in the *Shan Hai Jing*. This may also be true of the mounds and large visible ancient symbols in the Eastern United States.

[4] Definite Chinese influence

[5] With the present increase in tourism the Yiu-Yiu must be having an amazing come-back of popularity.

[6] Millet is an ancient Chinese food. We had it often for breakfast when I was a child in Henan province. This shows another strong proof of Chinese occupancy of early America.

[7] Notice the mention of horses. Remember, Alaska (Dah Han) sent horses as tribute to China, in ancient times. Many scientific "certainties" as to what ancient America did not have ... may be completely mistaken.

[8] We are immediately reminded of the identification cauldrons of Emperor Yu. Was there a place-cauldron left here? The question intrigues us.

[9] Henriette Mertz has verified nearly all these places, and found them accurate as to descriptions and distances. See her excellent book, *Pale Ink.*

[10] Fourteenth Book of *Shan Hai Jing*. These were bird clans, of Chinese origin.

[11] Jade horses of a green color were beloved by ancient Chinese. The Mexican jadeite must have been a rare treat to Chinese who only had nephrite jade.

[12] They were there until the Conquest. The fruits and flowers are still wonderful.

[13] It seems highly likely Emperor Yao allowed Huan Tow to bury him in Yucatan beside his beloved friend, Huan Doe.

[14] It is not uncommon for Chinese actors, or religious showmen, to appear, in early times, with several heads, tails, "Legs," etc. I have seen examples of these multi-headed figures in Chinese paintings.

[15] This suggests Asian contact.

[16] When poets calculate distances, and clergymen report audiences, there is a tendency toward a slight exaggeration.

[17] The fact that the "Black people" ate rice should cause us no perplexity when we remember who their forefathers were.

[18] Shu-Hai is another Chinese American Indian Nation.

[19] This probably has astronomical significances.

[20] Note by Rees— It says that they made their clothes from water animals. Possibly they made trousers from seal skins. That would give them the appearance of having black hips.

[21] A persistent fear of baths and a nearness to oil lamps may have produced an artificial blackness that seemed not only odoriferous but ancestral.

[22] The Ancient Chinese were practical as well as lyrical, and here plainly say they did not really think the sun and moon rose out of the Grand Canyon.

[23] Notice this early interchange between China, Korea and Japan, and their joint concern for "America."

[24] Once again the Chinese connection is apparent in the use of millet.

[25] These are possibly tribal divisions of the Mogollons.

[26] The Chinese greatly admire moral purity

[27] Emperor Thang-Ti lived 2640 B.C. We are forced to accept the probability that his son Prince Yu-Kwoh, and his grandson Yu-King fathered and controlled two islands or districts such as Hokkaido in the North and Vancouver island in the east. To deify them, after a few years, would be as natural to the ancient Chinese as reaching for a bowl of rice.

[28] It is my personal conviction that the Northern Sea (in *Shan Hai Jing* usage) is the ocean from Hokkaido to Alaska—the Eastern Seas is the Pacific—with special emphasis on the American coast—and that the South Sea is the Pacific South of California, with some emphasis on the Gulf of California.

[29] Yiu-I seems to have been a prince before he was forced to flee. Having the artificial long head of the nobility it is understandable that the women of the Land of Women—where he fled, and who were probably his daughters, would also have the long aristocratic head still found in the figurines of Baja maidens.

[30] Hi or Hsi seems to have had a rich history. He was almost everybody's father. His own father was Emperor Shun. Hsi was father of the first "American" Quakers! (see above).

[31] Nu-Cheu's body is probably a statue of a beautiful long-headed woman. Look for it!

[32] This account of the Kih Yung Horses ("North-east beyond the sea") agrees with the Dah Han (Alaska) traditions of fine horses there.

[33] Yuen "controlled" the Sun and Moon. It is easy to see how. "The people that control the darkness" might have been his descendants. This is one of the clear proofs of the ancient Chinese observatory system at the Grand Canyon. This is carried on until now by the Hopis. This Yuen seems to have operated as an astronomer and meteorologist, probably on the official Imperial Chinese orders.

[34] "Uncle Dragon" land is north of the canyon on the Harris Fu Sang map.

[35] Vining, p. 678

Bibliography

[Note: Chinese names below were left in the order they are normally spoken since surnames are first.]

"Ancient Chinese Coins Found," *The Weekly Colonist*, Victoria B.C., October 25, 1852.

Ashe, Geoffrey, Thor Heyrdahl, Helge Ingstad, J.V. Luce, Betty J. Meggers, and Birgitta L. Wallace, *The Quest for America*, London: Pall Mall Press, 1971.

Bancroft, Hubert Howe, "History of the Northwest Coast," *Works*, Vol.1, 1884.

Bazin, M., *Journal Asiatique*, 1839.

Beaglehole, J. C., *The Exploration of the Pacific*, London: A.C. Black. Ltd, 1934.

Bernal, Ignacio, *Mexico Before Cortez—Art, History, and Legend*, Dolphin Books, 1972.

Bloomgarden, Richard, *Mexico City, Archaeological Sites and Museums*, Publicado e impreso por Litografica Turmex, S.A.

Boyd, William C., *Genetics and the Races of Man*, Boston: Little, Brown and Co., 1950.

Burland, C.A., *The Ancient Maya*, 5 Winsley St., London, W.1: Weidenfeld and Nicolson (Educational) Ltd., 1967.

Burland, Cottie, *North American Indian Mythology*, Feltham, England: Hemlyn Publishing Group, 1970.

Chao-Shi, *Commentary on the Chronicle of the Kingdoms of Wu and Yue.*

Chapman, Charles. E., *A History of California—The Spanish Period*, New York: Macmillan, 1921.

Chau Ju Kua, *Chu Fan Chi.*

Chavannes, E., translation of *The Historical Memoirs of Se-Ma-Tsien*, 1895.

China News, Taipei, Taiwan, January 14, 1969.

Coe, Michael D., *The Maya*, Penguin Books, Ringwood, Victoria, Australia, 1971.

Consideration of the Western and Southern Kingdoms, (Late Han Dynasty Publication).

Couling, Samuel, Editor, *The New China Review* ((Vols. 1 to 4), Taipei: Republished by Literature House, 1919-1922.

De Dioses, Lugar, *Teotihuacan, Espanol, English, Francais, Artes De Mexico*, Mexico, 1970.

De Saussure, Par Leopold, *Les Origines De L'Astronomie Chenoise*,Taipei: Cheng Wen Publishing Company, 1967.

Dictionary of Expressions, Taiwan, 1970.

Durant, Will, *Our Oriental Heritage*, New York: Simon and Schuster Co., 1954.

Dz Hai, Taipei, 1972.

Ekholm, Gordon, and Gordon Wiley, Editors, *Archeological Frontiers and External Connections* (Four Vols.), Austin: University of Texas Press, 1966.

Fite and Freeman, Editors, *A Book of Old Maps Delineating American History*, New York: Daven Publication, Inc., 1969.

Fleming, Thomas, "Who Really Discovered America," *Reader's Digest*, April 1973.

Forbes, Jack D., *The Indian In America's Past*, Englewood Cliffs, New Jersey: Prentice Hall Inc., 1964.

Gaubil, Pere, "Letters," *Noveau Journal Asiatique de Paris*, Vol. X.

Gordon, Cyrus H., *Before Columbus*, New York: Crown Publishing, 1971.

Hanke-Little, Lewis, *The Spanish Struggle for Justice in the Conquest of America*, Little, Brown and Company (Canada) Ltd., 1965.

Hapgood, Charles, *Maps of the Ancient Sea Kings*, New York: Chilton Books, 1966.

Harris—Fu Sang Map Book, Copy of a revised Shan Hai Jing map, plus Korean maps of early times, and an ancient Japanese map. Seoul, Korea.

Hawkes, David, *Ch'u Th'u, The Songs of South* (an ancient Chinese anthology), Oxford, 1957.

Helfritz, Hans, *Mexican Cities of the Gods*, Verlag D. Schanberg, Koln, Co., 1968.

Hirth, Friedrich and W.W. Rockhill, *Chau-Ju-Kua*, (Chinese and Arab Trade, twelfth and thirteenth centuries), Translated from the Chinese and annotated, St. Petersburg Printing Office of the Imperial Academy of Sciences, 1911.

Hulbert, H.E., "An Ancient Map of the World," *American Geographic Society*, October 1904.

Ionides, Margaret L. and Stephen A. Ionides, *Stars and Men*, Indianapolis, Indiana: Bobbs-Merrill, 1939.

I Tsing, *A Record of the Buddhist Religion as Practiced in India and the Malay Archipelago* (A.D. 671-695), Oxford: Claredon Press, 1896.

James, G. W., *In and Around the Grand Canyon*, Boston: Little, Brown and Co., 1908.

Kia Tan, *Hai-wei-hoa-yi-thou*, (Map of the Celestial Empire and the Barbarian Countries within the Seas), 730-805 A.D.

Kai-Yu, *The Familiar Discourses of Confucius*.

Klaproth, M., *Nouvelles Annales des Voyages*, 1831.

Koeman, I. C., *Joan Bleau and His Grand Atlas*, Amsterdam: George Philip & Son, 1972.

Kun Yuen, *"Lisao,"* Third Century B.C.

Larson, Robert, "Was America the Wonderful Land of Fu Sang?" *American Heritage*, Vol. 17, April 1966.

Legge, Rev. James, *The Notions of the Chinese Concerning God and Spirits*, Hong Kong: Hong Kong Register Office, 1852.

Leland, Charles G., *Fu Sang*, New York: J.W. Bouton, 1875.

Leonard, Jonathan Norton, *Ancient America*, Time Inc., Morristown, New Jersey: Silver Burdett Co., 1967.

Liu-siu, *Canon of the Five Chan-Kings*, Tcheou Dynasty. (Compilation by Liu-siu, who added *Hai-wei-king* and *Hai-new-king*, before A.D. 57).

Mason, O. T., *Smithsonian Reports*, 1894.

Meng-Kien, Editor, *Shan Hai Ching, Book of the Mountains and the Seas*, (AKA, *Shan Hai King, Shan Hai Jing*).

Mertz, Henriette, *Pale Ink*, Chicago, Illinois, 1953.

Morley, Sylvanus G., *The Ancient Maya*, Stanford, Calif.: Stanford University Press, 1972.

Moule, Arthur Evan, *The Chinese People*, London, 1914.

Nakamura, Hiroshi, "Old Chinese World Maps Preserved by the Koreans," *Mapa Mundi, Vol. 4.*

Needham, Joseph, *Clerks and Craftsmen in China and the West*, Cambridge, England: Cambridge University Press, 1970.

——, *Science and Civilization in China*, (Five Volumes), University of Cambridge, Chinese Reprint, Taipei, 1970.

Prescott, William H., *Mexico and the Life of the Conqueror Fernando Cortez*, (Two Volumes), P.F. Collier and Son, New York 1902, (part of the "Nations of the World" set of books).

Ramsey, Raymond H., *No Longer on the Map*, New York: Viking Press, 1972.

"Sacred Writings," *Harvard Classics*, Vol. 2, New York: Collier Press, 1910.

Shau Wing Chan, *English-Chinese Dictionary*, Second Edition, Stanford, Calif.: Stanford University Press, 1968.

Shui King, (Book of the Waters).

Shan King, (Book of the Mountains).

Sih Mah Gwan, *The Sung Dynasty TZ Jih Taeng Jan* (Chou to Tang History), Vol. 176, Taipei: Wen Gwang Bookstore, 1972.

Skelton, R.A., *Explorer's Maps*, Spring Books, Hong Kong: Lee Fung Printing Co., 1970.

Soothill, William Edward and Lewis Hodus, *A Dictionary of Chinese Buddhist Terms*, Kegan, Paul, Trench, Trubner & Co., London, Taipei Reprint: Chen Wen Publishing Co., 1970.

Spiden, Herbert Joseph, *Maya Art and Civilization*, Indian Hill, CO.: Falcon Wing Press, 1957.

The Holy Bible, King James Version.

Tso-sse, *Wu-tu-fu*, (Verse of the Five Capitals).

Students English-Chinese Dictionary, Taipei, 1970.

Vaillant, G. C., *The Aztecs of Mexico*, Bungay, Suffolk, Great Britain: Doubleday, Doran and Co., 1960.

Verrill, Alpheus Hyatt and Ruth Verrill, *America's Ancient Civilizations*, New York: Putnam, 1953.

Vlahos, Olivia, "Indian Cultures in the Americas,"*New World Beginnings*, Greenwich, Conn.: Fawcett Publishers, 1972.

Vining, Edward, *An Inglorious Columbus: or Evidence that Hwui Shan and a Party of Buddhist Monks from Afghanistan Discovered America*, London: D. Appleton and Company, 1885.

Von Hagen,Victor W., *Realm of the Incas*, New American Library, New York: Mentor Books,1957.

——, *World of the Maya*, New America Library, New York: Signet Books, 1960.

Waley, Arthur, *The Way and Its Power*, New York: Grove Press Inc., 1958.

Werner, E.T.C., "A Note on Head-Flattening," *New China Review*, Vol. 1, 1919.

Whiteside, Professor Joseph, Editor, *Outline of Chinese History*, Shanghai: Li Ung Bing, 1914.

Williams, Rt. Rev. Channing M., "Letter," *Magazine of American History*, April, 1883.

Wright, Barton and Evelyn Roat, *This Is a Hopi Kachina*, Flagstaff, Arizona: Museum of Northern Arizona, 1970.

Wylie, Alexander, *Chinese Researches*, Shanghai, 1897.

Yi Ik-Seup, "A Map of the World," *The Korean Depository*, Vol. 1, 1892.